PIRENE'S
FOUNTAIN

PIRENE'S FOUNTAIN

Senior Editor	Lark Vernon Timmons
Submissions and Review Editor	Elizabeth Nichols
Design & Layout Editor	Steve Asmussen
Associate Editors	Royce Hamel Linda E. Kim Paul Kim Kelly Cressio-Moeller
Web Editor	Katherine Herschler
Art Consultant	Tracy McQueen
Editor & Publisher	Ami Kaye

Pirene's Fountain
Tenth Anniversary Issue

Volume 11, Issue 19

Pirene's Fountain: A Journal of Poetry
Volume 11, Issue 19
Copyright © 2018 Pirene's Fountain
Paperback ISSN 2331-1096

Layout, Book & Cover Design: Steven Asmussen
Copyediting: Elizabeth Nichols & Linda E. Kim
Cover Artist: Tracy McQueen
Photo, p. 85: Carlo Pizzati

All rights reserved: except for the purpose of quoting brief passages for review, no part of this book may be reproduced or transmitted in any form or by any means, electronic or mechanical, including photocopying, recording, or by any information storage and retrieval system, without permission in writing from the publisher.

Glass Lyre Press, LLC
P.O. Box 2693
Glenview, IL 60025

www.GlassLyrePress.com

Dear Readers,

What a pleasure it is to welcome you to this milestone edition of *Pirene's Fountain*—**it's our tenth anniversary, and we are still learning!**

Tracy McQueen's vibrant rendering of "Gaia" graces the cover of our special issue; we extend our appreciation and gratitude to our fine list of contributors as well.

It was my privilege to showcase the multi-talented Tishani Doshi, whose feature also includes her conversation with Ami Kaye. In addition, we offer Andrea Witzke Slot's book review of Shanta Acharya; Elizabeth Nichols' reviews of John Amen and Beth Copeland; and Linda E. Kim's reviews of Linda Ashok and Judith A. Skillman.

Pirene's Fountain is the brainchild of Ami Kaye, who befriended her original international cast of characters online in 2008, and shepherded us to the delivery of *Pirene's* first digital issues.

The establishment of Glass Lyre Press in 2012 widened the scope of writing we could bring our readers by giving contributors the opportunity to submit their work for print publication.

In keeping with our philosophy of inclusion and desire to contribute to the greater good, *Pirene's* publications—Japan anthology (*Sunrise from Blue Thunder*), World Peace (*Carrying the Branch*), and *Collateral Damage* — all continue to benefit global concerns, and provide a way to show solidarity.

Coming up, our 2019 *Pirene's Fountain* issue features culinary poems. We invite you to join our Facebook poetry group for details and updates.

In closing, we are indebted to our loyal readership and all the talented individuals who have contributed to *Pirene's Fountain* in the last decade—this anniversary issue is dedicated to you!

Sincerely,
Lark Vernon Timmons
Senior Editor, *Pirene's Fountain*

Contents

Poetry

Shanta Acharya
    KABUL: 14th November 2001   13

Sofiul Azam
    What Could Have Happened on a
        Spring Afternoon?   14

Sofia A. Bening
    Nuit   15

Margo Berdeshevsky
    Before The Hunger Of Silk Worms   16

Sharon Chmielarz
    Thyme   18

Joan Colby
    Contemplating the Owl   19

Rachel Dacus
    Aurora Borealis   21

Yoko Danno
    Drinks Today   22

Lori Desrosiers
    Blur   23

Tishani Doshi
    Disco Biscuits   24

Lisken Van Pelt Dus
    Ode to the Universe   25

Diane Frank
    Under a Copper Moon   26

Marc Frazier
    Stories, Cafe Voltaire   27

Madeline Gardiner
    Three   28

Gail Goepfert
    Kahlo Images: White on Canvas   29

Grace Marie Grafton
    Ladder (4)   30

Timothy Green
    Pre-Existing Conditions   31

Hedy Habra
    Or What is Life if not a Constant Carving
        of Oneself?   32

Mary Hutchins Harris
    At the widening   33

Melinda B Hipple
    Earthquake   34

James Croal Jackson
    Meditation On Muscle Memory   35

Trish Lindsey Jaggers
    Ars Longa, Vita Brevis   36

Laurie Kolp
    Cradle-curled Leaf   37

Desmond Kon and Eric Valles
    Dream of the Window Soul: Behold de Man   38

Rustin Larson
    The Great Mother's Gift to Us   39

Marie Lecrivain
    momento microaggression   40

Peter Ludwin
    Archetype   41

Dennis Maloney
    The Summer I Learned What Work Was   43

Jennifer Martelli
    Northern Long-Eared Bats on the Pipeline Route   44

Libby Maxey
    Domine, exaudi   45

Ken Meisel
    Rose Mallow (Representation)   46

Cameron Morse
    Leaving Colorado   48

Robbi Nester
    Questions   49

Karen Neuberg
    Encuentro   51
Aimee Nezhukumatathil
    Chess   52
    Penguin Valentine   53
Cristina M. R. Norcross
    The Continent of My Belly   54
M. Nasorri Pavone
    Missing the Eclipse   55
Jared Pearce
    I've Been Wondering Where   56
Paul Perreault
    Just to Leave the House   57
Pina Piccolo
    Shadows of Paris   58
    Ombre Di Parigi   61
Thomas Piekarski
    Why We Rhyme   64
Connie Post
    Dancing with the Father   65
Tree Riesener
    environmental issues   66
Claire Donohue Roof
    If This is Us   67
Beate Sigriddaughter
    Strawberry Ledge Forever   68
Joannie Stangeland
    Leave   69
Tim Suermondt
    The Last Train Leaves The Station   71
Susan Tepper
    correspondence from a different war   72
Jon Tribble
    The Dining Hall   75
Pamela Uschuk
    HOLOGRAMS   77
Helen Wickes
    Ambition, Late Life   78

Martin Willitts, Jr.
      Sonnet: Black and White Octaves   79
Kath Abela Wilson
      Her Wish   80
Bill Yarrow
      Self Inventory   81

Showcase

Tishani Doshi: Time, Rhythm
      & the Luxury of Slowness   85
In Conversation with Tishani Doshi   95

Reviews

Blue Honey by Beth Copeland   100
Illusion of an Overwhelm by John Amen   104
Imagine: New and Selected Poems by
      Shanta Acharya   110
Kafka's Shadow by Judith Skillman   114
whorelight by Linda Ashok   119

Publication Credits

Contributor Notes

POETRY

KABUL: 14TH NOVEMBER 2001

Shanta Acharya

Standing in front of the mirror
combing back his hair, he encounters
a long-lost friend, a stranger,
never having seen his face without a beard
except when too young to remember.

His face looks gaunt though finely chiselled
in rock, the skin smooth and shining,
melting ice. He has tasted honey in freedom,
having discarded his facial mask.

It took the barber in the market an hour
to retrieve his face from beneath the rubble
of beard, five years of forbidden fruit.

His wife hums in the kitchen, immersed
in the ceremony of making tea —
singing to tunes playing on the radio
which has also emerged from purdah.

Her long raven hair declares liberty,
resplendent testimony in the setting sun,
her face smiling after an eternity —
she is expecting their first baby.

His gaze is glued to her face in the mirror.

She has never known peace in her time,
nor could he remember what it was like
when men grew old and the land was green.

In the distance bombs keep shattering
the silence of the surrounding ruins.

What Could Have Happened on a Spring Afternoon?

Sofiul Azam

I should have kissed you on a spring afternoon
when there was a gust of wind ruffling your unbound hair.
Your eyes didn't have the stony stare, and the sunlight fell on you
– streaking through smudged, south-facing windowpanes –
to add up to the beauty of your unpainted face.
I was looking at you and anxiously thinking of you.
Were you thinking of what I was thinking about?
You teasingly squeezed orange peels into my eyes.
I suspect your chest was heaving too much like waves
with the anticipation of what would follow next. Many things

could have happened: I could have you roped off by love –
the most tightening, though a little frightening,
of all ropes in the world. I could have held you
the way the destitute do their bundles of last things before guns.
I could have entered you the way ancient men entered caves
to save themselves from the outside world's insecurity
for I never wanted an eavesdropper's booze or bolster
on a lonely bed. I didn't have a good-for-nothing's supinity
or a namedropper's vanity. Yet only I could have
made you a river by jumping into you. But I shrugged off

each of the options carefully like an intelligent fool,
thinking I was stepping dangerously beyond borders,
awaiting snipers' bullets out of nowhere. I remember your eyes
about to come alive with the tide of your tears
and your lips quivering to word a timid sentence with love.
Maybe time was against us, and finally it has wedged
a gulf widening ever more in between us and set us
two separate islands far apart on our different courses.
And now there's nothing else for me to get past being terrified
except one thing at last – a poem punctuated by regrets.

NUIT

Sofia A. Bening

"...she was mine, the key was in my fist, my fist was in my pocket, she was mine."
— *Vladimir Nabokov,* Lolita

spiral finger-pads
glide across gnarled granite edge
prick, burst red bubble

lone trickle glistens —
yes, offer it to la lune
she scorches the skin

melt like wax to bone
seep into the sodden ground
hope of a union.

Before The Hunger Of Silk Worms

Margo Berdeshevsky

> *"If a blackbird gets used to its name it cannot fly."*
> —Göksenur C.

In harem cages, the black doves free outside,
did a quiet woman sing in her bath while her hair was
brushed by a man with knife-sliced testes? Did the heat in her
sultan's penis ever please her? Did she sing in her sleep
with the mulberry's worms?

Don't listen to exhales from your city on the shore
of a throat of water, don't listen any more to prayer that's
a boa rising from the muezzin's basket—don't
listen because you may have stopped believing,

mother in a green full belly shift how you whisper *come
to the land of the mulberry,* and you mean don't listen to it
falling, mean don't listen to the blood of your unannounced
infant, head crowning into fingers in the middle of summer.
Your land of prayer calls between baritone and caterwaul.

I'm listening to a sea outside
where odalisques couldn't swim,
the sound of their stone baths chilling.
I've come to a land
and I'm listening to names
and I'm listening to the mulberry

listening to buried women whispering
the musk of their own sex,
patient for its night of once a month use.
The raw flesh of a woman used too often.

A country's black eye cutting open
a metal rain, one border, closing.
One coquette-boy's epileptic
shimmy for a table of women.

I'm listening to a princess in her father's island prison
—locked in to escape her cradle-side curse. Killed by
a snake in a basket of apples on her eighteenth birthday.
I'm listening to the Golden Horn, mourning her, still.

Where is that
mulberry? Who splayed it into bloom?
I want to listen to its leaves before they are eaten.
Resist. Before the hunger of silk worms.

THYME

Sharon Chmielarz

Old, single-syllable word with an old-fashioned *th* beginning, an ancient consonant-compound that lodges back of front teeth and turns an *h* under tongue-pressure into common *ta* to usher out a quaint *Y*, sounding just like long *i* today. – A trick older than a hand-made lace collar that startles the dark bodice it circles. Elegant in form, *Y* is totally at home mid-word as a tool in its chest. Neighbor to *M*, a favorite human sound which floats away with the silent *e*. A miracle the *e* hasn't been dropped; it's a gnomic little happiness defending the presence of the useless. A tale in nothingness. Whether recognized or not, the *e* hangs on for dear life. Inaudible as fragrance. Maybe carrying an important message from silence.

CONTEMPLATING THE OWL

Joan Colby

The wisdom of the owl
Infects your dream. Its claws
Riddled with the filth
Of ages. Athenians thought
Destiny could be divined
From its innards. That bespoken
Owl of imagery seen
Gliding out of the dark
Into the bedroom where sleepers
Clutch each other like field mice.
The eagle-owl, monstrous in its wingspan,
Flies straight at you, careless one,
Strolling after midnight
Intent on stars. It's true,
We are all starlight, fragments
Of a great eruption
That spread its vast wings
Through the universe. Now,
In the colonnades of ancient ruins,
The owl invests a querulous nobility
In your credulity. This is the city
Of the mind
Where the owl hunts nightly,
Its ghost face accosting you,
Its beak, that horror,
Swallowing the world you sought.
The world of mercy. The world of deliberation.
Listen, the owl is sudden,
Its genius is surprise. Its creed
Not wise, but famished.
It knows nothing, nothing
Of cruelty or pity.
Goddess of the immaculate city
You tear our hearts into this debris,
Vomitus of all we learned,

Our tenuous civilization
Gripped in talons unconcerned
With anything but the survival
Of the nest and the brood
And the feeding.

Aurora Borealis

Rachel Dacus

She heard the green curtains of light
crackle in the stillness
as she skied home from school,
snow squeaking under her.
A girl growing up near the Arctic Circle,
my stepmother heard phone lines sing
as they froze and tightened.

The early-orphaned child
whose siblings were sent away
trekked the country alone,
humming back in a whisper
to the wires' harmonics.
She had learned never to speak much,
but to do it in many languages.

Silence now invades her elder brain.
She can't always remember my father,
but she can describe skiing
under that midnight sun
and later a year living in Rome,
the daily pasta and *Ciao bella*,
when she worked as a script girl
on Fellini's crew making *La Dolce Vita*.

Smiling her wren's smile, she says
she misses her oceanside home
and my father. Their sweet life
and the roses she grew. After he died,
we moved her north to us.
She tells my brother she doesn't know
if she ate today but then tells me
about Sweden's snowflakes
forming crystalline on her eyelashes.

Drinks Today

Yoko Danno

a stranger standing at the back door
of my house asked for a bowl of herb
tea ? for years, he said, he's been trying
to sing after his vocal cords were excised

*

i drank green tea & orange juice,
and finally finished with red wine

*

autumnal leaves tinged my brain,
"don't sleep in the rain, my dear"

*

finding no exit from my tangled-up dreams,
i stumbled down the stairs to the platform ?

    the train goes round and round
    on the circle line as if intoxicated

BLUR

Lori Desrosiers

used to be a photograph
colors faded by water
human-shaped

who took this
from whose house
is it still there

were they able to salvage
the walls, did they tear out
the sheetrock, the wood floors

the soaked carpet
the children's blocks
floating out the door

pots and a toaster
bouncing on water
like a tiny boat parade

which flood did this
and did the people
in the photo survive

DISCO BISCUITS

Tishani Doshi

We were talking about the subject of Quaaludes, of which I know nothing except back in the 70s, when I was being born, Bill Cosby slipped them to a bunch of women. When I think of the past like that I think of a child hiding under the staircase among the family's dusty shoes, a pair of discontented lampshades. How most of us have known a man who arrived like Bill—sleek and proud as a July thunderstorm. How so many of us gave in to that sleekness because when you're young you don't know that your bones have been giving way the second you were born. So you give, and your giving's large and uncalculated. But then there's the haunting. And how it works is a kind of time warp that bitch-slaps you when you're at your innocent best, like this morning, in the dance theatre, which is all mongoose-hurry, ant-scurry, and slow slowing down. I was going for that out of body experience with navel to floor, toes to ceiling. I heard the sap rise in the frills of those indefatigable shrubs, the crows going on with their cawing, the sea in the distance, beautiful in her reiterations. I heard time cracking at his knees, and suddenly, kablam. I'm seventeen, trudging home. The church at the corner is folding in on itself, a mendicant struggles with the flaps of his loincloth. Even the lampposts are desperate to tuck in their ungainly feet. All of us have something to hide. The city and her persiflage. The acres of burning sand. Listen now, as the wind caterwauls like a deranged megaphone. All our old selves are parading the beach, whispering how there should be a museum for this kind of installation. They're crushing bits of nostalgia in their heels. They grow photophobic and bendy. They splinter. They shirr.

Ode to the Universe

Lisken Van Pelt Dus

Because, why not? oh most
opalescent everything, mine
for every known mineral,
every unknown element, every
imaginable oh, and then some.

Because you're the only modest
proof we have of, well, almost
anything. Maybe not so modest –
enormity inviolate, embodied,
a giantess, beyond our mortal scope.

Because you birth horizons, mermaids,
muddy brooks, black holes.
Because of silver, magnets, homes.

Because I've loved in you, whole lifetimes,
moved by the smell of hazelnut
or dough rising, roused by a lifting
murmur – *do, re, mi* – as I were
tuning fork, song in motion.

Because you let the moon foreshadow us –
our growth, our fall, our need for orbit.
Because you hold us, hold us, every molecule.

Under a Copper Moon

Diane Frank

After the storm, a dream buffalo
nested in our yard
surrounded by lavender.

Buffalo clouds
thundering on the horizon.

Clouds like white turtles
crawling across a wide lake of sky,
blue and shimmering.

When a buffalo enters your dream,
listen for arpeggio hooves,
the weight of music,
a copper moon
above a vanishing prairie.

Timpani of thunder pounding red clay,
the weight of time.
The light at the edge of the universe.

STORIES, CAFE VOLTAIRE

Marc Frazier

The solstice is almost here. I wrote a poem by that title.
It was about loss, which surprised no one.
I almost mailed you a book. About loss. But also salvation.
The woman goes home with her baby. On a train.
To her father. Everyone is damaged but alive.
Except her husband who dies in an auto wreck.
If I mail you the book, I will not show you this poem until later.
I am surprised I told you the ending.
I wanted to hear it for some reason, though I am discomfited by it.
These days my mind works farther and farther ahead of itself:
a plot line gone haywire.
The author's voice is the ocean echoing along shore

bearing some inevitability I cannot accept.

Another ending disturbs me: a woman, American, dazed from experience,
heat, leaves her cab and wanders into the maze of a North African town.
The people who've come to retrieve her discover she is gone.
She does not want to be saved.
Which is more disquieting: that this is no ending,

or that I understand why she does it?

The woman next to me is bald. By choice.
I think of chemo patients who dream hair.
Across from her is a man who writes frantically in a book,
scribbles between line after line of copyrighted print.
I think of the author, how critical each word was,

how one way, or another, we make stories fit.

THREE

Madeline Gardiner

My father's boots and me in the log cabin,
snow everywhere piling down.
My dark bangs like drapes across my face's window-
it's here where my father knows how to love.
With open hearth the risky tumbler
pulls me from his leather tromps and throws me
my head inches from the ceiling fan
my eyes dark coals inside my head
my backbone made of iron
and blooming around me
my blue dress a gas turning blaze
waggish wings and matchstick legs
ready to catch a lighter's flame again.

Kahlo Images: White on Canvas

Gail Goepfert
—after Ruth Stone

A white bedsheet, whiter
soaked with blood, white pelvis
bone crushed.

White lace-trimmed
skirts, white toilet seat,
lid back, white lace gloves.

Schoolgirl uniform
blouse, one human arm
projecting from sleeve.

Broken conch shell,
white, white
skyscraper erupting from
volcano.

A sugar skull,
pale white moon. White
magnolias.

White rind of watermelon
and orange, tight white lace ruff
about the face.

White
lace umbrella against
a cerulean sky.

Still-life
of bleached halved papaya,
splayed and seedless.

LADDER (4)

Grace Marie Grafton

When the poppy closes its eye at night, it misses
the face of the moon. We humans are fools for
the full moon, its shameless friendliness. But the poppy,
pridefully, has decided to protect her splendid dress
from the cold white she believes will steal her gold.

Xylophone notes carry on the echo tradition, rounding
out human ear canals, reminding us how hollows
can provide protection for shyer beauty, vulnerable
youth. We notice how tones swirl, expand, linger
in the interstices between our skulls' bony plates.

In afternoon's remedy hangs the drying laundry
gathering the spell of sun's promise to keep us alive.
Two jays' impetuous squawks, quick ladybug's aproned
inspection of larkspur's frothy leaves. Afternoon imprints
squirreled away in sheets that will cover our bed.

Invite the impetuous, remember it is said that
bouncing clears the lymph system, think of
ballet dancers' leaps, the almost-flight, think
of birds, how their flit-flit lifts sluggish blood.
Let's go swimming in fog's shocking chill.

In fairy tales, the woman tending the spinning wheel
is usually portrayed as Mother or Grandmother, patient,
hard-working. But she is truly The One Who Knows How
To Transform. Give her fluff, it becomes thread, give her
thread, it becomes dress, give her seed, it becomes child.

Pre-Existing Conditions

Timothy Green

I checked the box for "Other," and I tried
explaining how the protoplanetary
disk was like a node on a string inside
of space itself, a fretboard played by barely

randomness—I only meant the math
of orbital stability, of course—
and I'd describe accretion as a bath
of stardust, bombardment as Morse

code on the moon's beleaguered face,
the rocks outgassing oxides, the boiling
peptides caught in a lipid chain's embrace—
and on and on like acid strands uncoiling

eloquent as ancient ocean's spume—
but the insurance form was short: No room.

Or What is Life if not a Constant Carving of Oneself?

Hedy Habra

    And isn't happiness a matter
        of instants, each a dance between
  chi and chaos, a flux and reflux, a tidal
wave, rising and receding?

    And aren't joy and sadness part
of the same equation, a fluid oscillation,
    forward/backward?

    Watch how the sand we write upon
        only scars for a moment. Water
soothes, erases memories, a way to wash
away our passage on earth.

    In the backyard of my mind
life passes like a meandering stream,
    water carries silt,

        licks riverbeds, tastes new shores,
    gathers remnants of words
grain by grain, bit by bit, sharp-edged
        syllables that smell of loss.

    Let's get drunk on dew at dawn,
watch how oleander glows
    under the blushing light.

AT THE WIDENING

Mary Hutchins Harris

of dawn, you cannot hear them
hushed in an ornamental tree,
holding, beneath their wings
in case the light does not
arrive without a day to stir
their hum at passing shadows,
yours, the spotted dog, the bird
whose blue makes them blink,
hived as they are inside of small,
keening for a faultless tone
to hold this day, this night
coming on so pink, so soon

EARTHQUAKE

Melinda B Hipple

Her body shimmers with silver coins
scattered about the layers of delicate color
gathered at her hips. "It starts in the feet,"
she explains, barefoot in front of the class.
After hours of instruction in *danse oriental,*
we are both spent and energized. "Concentrate
on your feet. Feel the earth begin to tremble.
Feel the vibration climb from your heels
to your ankles. Your knees. Your hips."

We feel nothing at first. Then the fast-twitch
muscle fibers in our calves and thighs
fire neurons from fatigue, begin to quiver.
We heed our bodies. Find our rhythm.
And slowly, a room full of coins
begins to sing.

Meditation On Muscle Memory

James Croal Jackson

If I had musical talent
I wouldn't write poems.

Guitar-grown fingernails.
Nimble strings.

There's no need
to lie. I couldn't bring myself to try

when my parents thought
it'd be a good idea for me
to take piano lessons.

I had Game Boy eyes
and the Final Fantasy theme on repeat.

My dad had already explained
the difference between basin wrench

and torque. Wasted an afternoon
taping leaking pipes.

Like many of his time
he knew plumbing, mechanics,
home improvement

then brought me into rooms with broken
machines. My mind was Mickey Mouse
spelling words and song,

not the kind to vivisect
a bird to learn the function.

All I knew were not even stories yet
and still my hands
sing few callouses.

ARS LONGA, VITA BREVIS

Trish Lindsey Jaggers

in response to Archibald MacLeish's "Ars Poetica"

Not true, MacLeish.
Bird words punctuate the still, leave, then arrive,
commas and dashes on oak limbs.

A poem must speak; its breath
just lift the lid of the inner eye, then cool
the drop gathered there.

Move, as a flower unspins, flings
yellow dust on dark legs and white wings.
Stir the air, petal by petal.

Stay, staccato notes dropped
branch by branch,
from tree to moonlit tree.

Stay, a birthmark on the mind. Not a stain.
But almost.

Eclipse, spread fingers between sight and sun;
world of blood blocked by skin.

Laugh, stretch inside the doorway, take up space.

Silence, no. There's still the mortar. And tick
of thirst. And groans from babies' moms.

Love, love us to death. Leaning grasses, switched
by briars. Dark slung across the sea.
Make us want to be.

Honest. Willing to lie for the sake of truth. And die.
That means, too.

CRADLE-CURLED LEAF

Laurie Kolp

carried in wind as crisp as white, starched shirt
worn by man who is late to work,

his gait a stretch from stride to stride
as he traipses down the walk on the street's right side

past the tattooed dude strolling along
swinging ear-bud wires, mouth moving in song

as a pony-tailed lady clad in pink yoga pants
jogs zigzag, her lean body caught in a slant

breezing on by the newspaper stand
where workers chug coffee before 8 comes to land

and this leaf of autumn color catches each one's eye
as for a second, their worries pass by

every concern about the day
for that brief moment, slips away

one piece of freedom, one red-orange leaf,
one simple peek, one glimpse of peace.

Dream of the Window Soul: Behold de Man

Desmond Kon and Eric Valles

Look, room within room. Paul de Man behind oriel window.
Listen, beyond the glass: the academic dissects metaphors.
No position, but for Rorty beside Rilke, gazing at the clerestory,
wondering how their subject, de Man, could be truly six feet under.
Death. Urban Pastorale. Inscribed. Four quatrefoils. Four vaults.
Displacement. Worpswede landscape. Tenacious. Double life.
Speak, Mirrorface of All Windows. Speak, Elegist of Readers.
"Your first wife needs dough." "Break the glass, boa deconstructor."

No shattering gaze, how Rorty plummets into Rilke's looking glass,
as de Man mirrors the unknowable like a calix holding flowers.
Look. No touching. Feel. Suprematist and Constructivist in fields.
Listen. The teacher plucks magic out of a text. Sorcerer grinning.
Against glass, Gabriel Marcel cups his ear. What mood shift now?
Eternal Death. Infinite Displacement. "Dear Window, Oh Mirror!"
In the room, de Man defers. Nazi apologist. Unfaithful lover.
What of truth, what of elegy? "Death is a linguistic predicament."

The interjected speech the poem ends on is a truncation of Paul de Man's famous remark: "Death is a displaced name for a linguistic predicament." This is the first collaborative poem penned by Eric Tinsay Valles and Desmond Kon Zhicheng-Mingdé, who co-created the new poetic form, anima methodi, in 2017. An anthology of the anima methodi is forthcoming in 2018.

The Great Mother's Gift to Us

Rustin Larson

A beach of naturalness greeting
the window and the rain.
Where it can, the radio will sing for
our protection. I now relate the day,
what it was like, and so we sang. Now
she stands singing and trouble-free.
They will ask, "Did she give the rain, note the sun,
make summer her gift to us,
our currency, our canvas?" We
are the words and window; spilling over
requires to be the fire
and the siren and the gooseberries'
flash of July's picnic full
of river copper and coin of rain.

MOMENTO MICROAGGRESSION

Marie Lecrivain

the bee lay on the concrete, shedding fuzz
and wing as the last bit of life left its
body. being allergic, the absence of buzz
and sting doesn't bother me, but this sits
uneasy in my soul, my apparent
lack of anguish over this tiny death.
why should i care, i ask, *about an errant
insect whose venom stops the flow of breath
and life as i know it?* i choose to walk
away, keen to continue on my way,
and forgo satori, but to my shock,
this death reverberates throughout my day,
disrupting normal discourse with cold tears,
and whispered pardons to defuse my fears.

ARCHETYPE

Peter Ludwin

(for Leonard Ludwin)

As for you, my minotaur,
I've tried augury, divination,
means ancient and new. Must I kill

to break the spell you cast? To swallow
life-saving fluid the cactus yields?
Winter has strangled my voice.

The maze: a murder of crows
drives me inside. Clew of twine
held fast—a lifelong habit—

I raise a torch fashioned from rags and pitch.
My mind sees beyond oxygen-starved flame,
its sputter syncopated along the wall

until it reveals something that resembles you,
a shadow I graze with my finger.
Soft and wet, no snarl nor beastly features.

And eyes that implore, that demand a ticket home.
Where are the horns, the fearsome claws
that have always haunted my sleep?

Stumbling on a rock slick with excrement,
I lunge to save the torch jarred from my grip.
Stench envelopes me, a death cloud

makes me gag. Dizzy, I wonder:
What if I lay myself down between rocks
and old bones? Gave up a skin rouged

by thorns? But my sword hugs its scabbard.
Urgent now, I drag you to open air.
Who claims the minotaur? a voice

calls out. I do. The chimera already grows cold.
But where is the proof, the severed head?
On my tongue, I answer. A precious stone.

The Summer I Learned What Work Was

Dennis Maloney
for Phil Levine

The summer I learned what work was,
I was fourteen, the same age
as my oldest granddaughter,
working for 60 cents an hour
farm wage, when the regular
minimum was more than twice that.

I wanted a new bicycle and rode
my old one with the bad brakes
early each morning to a truck farm
at the ragged edge of the city where
houses petered out into small farms.

The crop rows seemed endless,
thinning lettuce seedlings, weeding
then bunching radishes, beets,
crawling along on my knees,
feeling the pain in my back
under a hot summer sun.

These days we drive through the
Salinas Valley, plumes from irrigation
sprays dance over the faint green lines.
Crops laid out in strict rows as far as the
eye can see to the hills on the horizon and
Mexican migrants bent over in the hot sun
picking the crops that will feed the nation
but we call that work by a different name.

Northern Long-Eared Bats on the Pipeline Route

Jennifer Martelli

Piled like D.H. Lawrence's odd left hand gloves, the bats

sleep high in their caves on the boreal line: above the waxy

junipers, the yew trees, the pines. Their suede ears,

a million times more subtle than ours, pick up the soft

stirring of the snakes knotted deep down in their hibernaculum

thawing, well past St. Brigid's Day. In their bat-dreams,

the snakes' hisses become a stream of gold milk from a warm teat,

tear of a defensive wound, a long slow leak serrating the air.

DOMINE, EXAUDI

Libby Maxey

I remember the time past;
   I muse upon all your deeds;
   I consider the works of your hands.
                          —Psalm 143:5

A chance of thunderstorms became your roof
collapsed, your house's face cracked open like
a crate, your clapboards puncturing the church.
The thaw uncovered beer cans in the ditch
just yesterday. Today, the litter's glass
and slates and chimney, porch and fences, barn.
The ruined hollow smells like Christmas in
the shadow of the shattered woods. It came
as a surprise, the morning—timely, through
the toppled avenues. The red-winged black-
birds, scattered, wonder where to congregate
to grind their sodden, warped calliope
for this too-early spring. The neighbors stoop
to gather, spreading out their hands.

Rose Mallow (Representation)

Ken Meisel

We are mirrors, says the rose mallow,
peaking up, and laying still and languid

on the water's vitreous surface
as I kneel to her, my camera in hand.

Her pallid white face, powdered,
softly streaked in chalk, in talc.

Her crimson lips, puckered in the center
like an Asian choral dancer –

blowing me a sensual, nameless kiss.
Her delicate hands, resting on water,

her thin streak of a body, submerged,
hidden, so that when I reach for her

she drifts away, and the birds above us,
rouse up, fly into the colors of a storm.

Think of every lover you have kissed,
every supple body, beneath your hand.

Is love the calling of the hidden organs –
bidding us to rise up for the first time

to test the harmony of our reach?
We are a formless circumstance –

testing what it feels like, to matter.
Look, she says, at the Japanese beetles

that consume my face, at the frogs
and snakes that use my body, for cover,

at the hummingbirds and bees that
offer their sweet pollen to my open lips.

We are representation, she says to me,
and we're just reflections for one another:

we're the sum of all our borrowings

Leaving Colorado

Cameron Morse

On the day before departure, I will ask
once more to hear the sound of Falling
River flowing through Estes Village
below my balcony rail, its *hush, hush,*

now. It's time to go. Once more observe
the clouds drape their giant shadows
over the alpine ridge, the black-streaked
clouds dragging white tassels over the saw

teeth of the pines. One more day and I might
have ascended through Douglas firs
to the black glacial lakes called Nymph,
Emerald, Dream, and spread out my body

for chipmunks and magpies to eat
one final vision out of my eyes:
That of you, my wife, the wind blowing
your black hair into my mouth.

QUESTIONS

Robbi Nester

As a child, I didn't spend much time

with my paternal grandmother.

I feared her hungry sidelong glance,

inspecting me, finding me wanting.

She denied any resemblance

others saw between us. But once

I spent a whole day at her house,

wishing she could be like other people's

grandmothers, warm and soft, uncritical.

Instead, she was all angles, small and spare,

like me. She seldom smiled.

At least she fed me. I remember eating

chicken soup out of a Wedgewood bowl.

I ate two helpings just for the joy

of getting to the bottom, where tiny

farmers tilled a field in blue and white,

all edged in willows and wild roses.

Along the bowl's steep sides, flocks of swallows

wheeled beneath white clouds and young girls

drove plump cows before them with a stick.

We didn't talk. I turned the pages of a picture book

distracted by the questions I would never ask.

Who were those people in the photographs

beneath the window? Why did my grandmother

find me such a disappointment? I knew I'd always

be an outsider, claimed and rejected, all at once.

ENCUENTRO

Karen Neuberg

after a painting by Remedios Varo

If blue it be/must be to lure
my eyes, to meet myself
as self, not girl, not separate
from now. Intact, we twirl
in cloth as swirl as sky
around, take form it gives
until my hollows fill
all my yearning years
within this shape of body.

Still I can't look away
and constantly peek back
into what held/still holds me
boxed & peering, in & out.
From here my soul
looks beyond and into sky.
And thus I go about
this hard business of living.

CHESS

Aimee Nezhukumatathil

Exactly four different men have tried
to teach me how to play. I could never
tell the difference between a rook
or bishop, but I knew the horse meant

knight. And that made sense to me,
because a horse *is* night: soot-hoof
and nostril, dark as a sabled evening
with no stars, bats, or moon-blooms.

It's a night in Ohio where a man sleeps
alone one week, and the next, the woman
he will eventually marry leans her body
into his for the first time, leans a kind

of faith, too—filled with white crickets
and bouquets of wild carrot. And
the months and the honeyed years
after that will make all the light

and dark squares feel like tiles
for a kitchen they can one day build
together. Every turn, every sacrificial
move—all the decoys, the castling,

the deflections—these will be both
riotous and unruly, the exact opposite
of what she thought she ever wanted
in the endgame of her days.

Penguin Valentine

Aimee Nezhukumatathil

Praise the patience of a papa penguin.
I don't envy those dark, starlit nights
with only the occasional blush-green
current of auroras across his claws.

See how sweetly he holds the egg close
in his brood pouch? And I am certain
his fierce tenderness would scare
even a crabeater seal five times his size.

What exactly does the papa penguin register
in a nighttime that lasts two whole months?
During those days of no sun, does he
remember the particular bend

of his mate's neck, what hint of yellow
near her ears? Or does he hunger for a slip
of hooked squid, worry the grand gulp of air
he must take, the concentration needed

to slow down his own heart? Praise
the faithfulness, the resolve, the lanceolate
feathers shaped like tiny spears, perfect
to poke through a cartoon heart and signal:

Valentine. And Valentine, I sing your praises
not because I know you'll wait for me
like that (though I know you would
if you could), but because you never waver.

I don't know how you know what direction
to look and how to listen for my return, even
when my call boils from the floor of the darkest
of arctic seas, even if, for now, all we can feel
is a cast of red crabs stretching before our path.

The Continent of My Belly

Cristina M. R. Norcross

When I was born
did I know that I would have
this many scars
across the continent
of my belly?

A map of stars –
ovary
ovary
uterus
ovary
ovary.

Connect the dots –
you will never find me.
These organs –
these sacred organs
of life
have left me.
I hold the stone of fertility
in my raw hands
like a pale blue robin's egg
about to fall
from its nest.

Thin shell,
liquid membrane –
return to the earth.

Missing the Eclipse

M. Nasorri Pavone

Missing the eclipse is good for those
tired of obstacles and their block of the light.

It depresses me to be reminded that even
the sun gets a black eye on cue.

You'll be dead when this one comes around again.
How could you have missed it? They asked.

I was distracted by something emotional
when I should have paid attention. *Shit.*

Isn't that how you wreck your car or
trip or how a knife slices you?

I missed my father's last breath by four minutes
so my mother could change her clothes,

so my sister could get there, as she handed off
her baby but not the car seat. Now she wishes

she hadn't watched. People are funny like that,
the big scramble to get their way: rushing,

shoving, breaking bones. *Move over, will you?*
I got here first. I'm trying to see the eclipse!

After they tackle you for the sale item, for the prize,
they may hold it up to the sky and conclude

that it really wasn't worth it. I hear that obstacles
can be overcome. They can also be overlooked.

I'VE BEEN WONDERING WHERE

Jared Pearce

     1
Harappan brick-makers, what did you
Talk about? The weaving girls' looks,
The mayor's plans for walls and drainage?
Did you envy the sailors, casting out
Onto terrible oceans and into weird ports?
Was it only your clay that consumed you?

Your priest-king and bosomed maids
Crumble in their age, and the careful tuning
Of your cities is now layered in dust
Alongside dead rivers. It was your heart
That built it all, but what built your heart?

Did you want to graffiti your bricks with
A copy of that delightful bronze seal? Did your God
Forsake you when you made no story for Him?

     2
Jaime's put me in charge of the ground,
But where will the trees, their various
species, end up? Will the corkscrew
willow fill-in the corner? Dogwood
or maple line old Forest Street?
Chestnut,
       kaleidoscopic canopy, rope
bridging you to us, you were here
when the street turned
to a number, when the Civil War
soldiers gimped home, when I planted
my homeless foot on your land,
allow me one center, one refuge—pinion
this spiraling planet so I can
build something to last.

Just to Leave the House

Paul Perreault

Lathered satisfaction
    scrub
    scrub
    scrubbing
        Between the fingers
        Under the nails

Rinse, repeat
Rinse, repeat
Rinse, repeat
Three times
    It's a Tuesday
    Threes are safe on Tuesdays

11 steps
to the kitchen
Bad number
Must check the locks on the back door again
            onetwothree
          bedroom
            onetwothree
          bathroom
            onetwothree

Front door
    tap
    tap
    tap on the doorknob

18 steps
from my door to my car

Six times three is eighteen
It's going to be a good day

Shadows of Paris

Pina Piccolo

7 January 2016

The trumpet's cry by the Seine
sounded like a buoy lamenting.
Blinded, it stumbled at the passage
of the *bateau-mouche*,
drunk with its lights displayed to the
greedy yearning of tourists.

He was there, squatting on a stool
between the shadowy grid of the bare
overhanging plane trees
and the moored houseboats with
overturned white tables awaiting summer.

Perhaps he was the shadow of Satchmo,
enchanted by invisible *ondines*,
since that March of 1965[1].
Every night he repeated the solo,
those notes of torment,
which now
float down
to the French Petite Afrique,
18th Arrondissement
at the foot of Montmartre,
the Goutte d'Or of the Chateau Rouge.

The notes now stuck to the black
skin of Adama, the Malian
Bambara, head of Security
at the Museum of Anthropology Quai Branly
"strongly desired by Jacques Chirac"
who, moving apace,
turns his back on

the fantastic blinding whiteness
of the Sacre Coeur,
which never stops atoning for the guilt
of the late 19th Century.

Stumbling over the mattress
of the newly homeless Dennis,
before being swallowed up
by the rapid organs of the city,
Adama turns upon hearing
the crackling sounds[2].

The shadow
has returned – he feels it in his bones –
the one that projects
powerfully and almost annuls
the other one from which whites,
for centuries, have been accustomed
to deflect their gaze.

It manifests itself at a frequency
almost invisible to western pupils,
producing a faint glimmer
perceptible to "other" optic nerves,
the frequency stamped on the wall
by trafficked weapons,
by fleet-footed Rimbaud,
sputtering victory
on the slopes of the Amba Alagi and Adua
while Menelik's drums covered
the trumpets of the retreating whiteness[3].

Now the neglected shadow
sneers and
takes refuge in the manuscripts
saved in Timbuktu, by Mamadou,
Adama's cousin.
Meanwhile, today in Paris, the other is the one shining,
It has become a blinding shadow,

in a simulated ring crazy
and full of rancor,
that flops to the ground
adding to the body count.

And yet the neglected shadow wanders
in the basements of the Louvre, amid
the new whiteness of the temple to the god Mac
and the ancient one of Hathor
stolen in a past
of glorious campaigns
on the backs of rearing white steeds.

While along the Seine
resumes the lamenting solo
of the shadow of Satchmo.
And in the vibration of the waves
dances the Amazon nymph
who arrived
a month ago
in the Sarayaku canoe[4]
to heal the waters.

Translated by Donald Stang and Pina Piccolo

[1]: Louis Armstrong gave a concert in Paris in March 1965.

[2]: On January 7, 2016, the anniversary of the Charlie Hebdo massacre in Paris, a Moroccan man wearing a suicide vest ("simulated ring" above) and carrying a meat cleaver appeared in front of the police station on the Rue de la Goutte d'Or shouting "God is great" in Arabic. He was shot down by police. Adama hears the shots.

[3]: Rimbaud became a gun dealer after his career as a poet. Guns he sold ended up in Menelik's hands and were used to defeat the Italian army in the battles of Adua and Amba Alagi.

[4]: The Amazonian Sarayaku tribe sailed a canoe up the Seine during a meeting on environmental protection in late 2015.

Ombre Di Parigi

Pina Piccolo

7 gennaio 2016

Lamento di boa mi era sembrato
la tromba che piangeva sul lungo Senna
accecata incespicava al passaggio
del bateau ebbro di luci
che le facciate rivelava
alla bramosia di turisti.

Stava lì accovacciato su uno sgabello
tra il reticolato di ombre
di platani spogli sovrastanti
e le dimore fluviali ormeggiate
su cui tavoli bianchi attendevano
l'estate capovolti.

Era forse l'ombra di Satchmo
stregata da invisibili ondine
da quel marzo del '65
Ogni sera ripeteva assolo
quelle note di strazio
che ora afflitte
galleggiavano là bas
sulla Piccola Africa
18th arrondisement
alla base di Montmartre
la Goutte d'Or de le Chateau Rouge

Attaccate, le note, alla pelle
negra di Adama, il maliano
bambara, capo della sicurezza
del museo di antropologia Quai Branly
"fortemente voluto da Jacques Chirac"
che di buon passo

lascia alle spalle
il candore fantasmeggiante
di quel Sacre Couer
che mai la smette di espiare le colpe
di fine diciannovesimo secolo

Inciampando sul materasso
del nouveau clochard Denis,
prima di essere inghiottito
dalle viscere veloci della città
si gira il bambara alla granicola
scoppiettante di suono

E' ritornata
l'ombra, lo sente nelle ossa,
quella che si proietta
potente e quasi annulla
l'altra quella da cui da secoli
les blancs sono abituati
a distogliere lo sguardo.

Si manifesta a una frequenza
quasi invisibile alle pupille occidentali
producendo un lieve baluginio
molto percettibile ad "altri" nervi ottici
quella stampata sul muro
dai fucili commerciati
da "suola al vento" Rimbaud,
crepitanti vittoria
sulle pendici di Amba Alagi e Adua
mentre i tamburi di Menelik coprivano
le trombe della nivea ritirata.

Disdegnosa ora ghigna
l'ombra negletta
e si rifugia nei manoscritti
salvati a Timbuctu, da Mamadou,
cugino di Adama.
Mentre, oggi a Parigi, brilla l'altra:

l'ombra accecante
nella cintura simulacro rancorosa
e folle stramazza nel conteggio.

Eppure si aggira ancora l'ombra trascurata
nei bassifondi del Louvre tra
il nuovo candore del tempio al dio mac
e quello antico di Hathor strappato
in un passato
di campagne gloriose
in groppa a bianchi destrieri impennati.

Mentre nel lungo Senna
riprende lamentoso l'assolo
dell'ombra di Satchmo.
E nel vibrare dell'onda
danza l'ondina amazzonica
arrivata
un mese fa
nella canoa Sarayaku
per guarire l'acqua.

WHY WE RHYME

Thomas Piekarski

Everybody has an axe to grind, but that doesn't necessarily suggest a ban on sharpening wheels or even sluice boxes. We plod ravines hoping that gold dust will float up from their willing waters. But bear in mind that when enriched rivers and streams have been dredged for centuries the gold becomes sparse. It's only in new, much higher ground, our atmospheric platitudes, dents in time, anatomical structures bold bells ring out. Therein is disclosed just why we rhyme.

Dancing with the Father

Connie Post

Now that you are dead
I can take two full breaths
and say

I didn't stand
on top of your feet
when we danced
in the living room

you stood
atop mine
and crushed my feet
like soft stone

you didn't tell me
how to follow the music
you followed me
until I had no music

you taught me
how to stand while broken
how to sit while bruised
how to run while bleeding
how to shut up during rape
how to kneel when cursed
and sing a broken church hymn
even while standing over you
in the grave silence

ENVIRONMENTAL ISSUES

Tree Riesener

*"...they see but half the universe
who have never been shown the house of pain."*
—*Emerson*

beside the rocky pool a warning
dangerous dam stand back from the boil

in landscape altered by snow
I drive through lost lanes and alleys
avenues and boulevards in need of bypass

in gardens we cry over the death of an oak
but cut grass without the slightest remorse

warm our hands at the stars
but drink the tears of crated pigs

although full of dna
skinflakes fingernail clippings
urine and blood
the earth cannot regenerate

but babies' feet are tender
soles that have not yet touched earth
little stomachs never distended
with long dead fat and gristle

lungs pink as not-yet-unfolded flower buds

still some hope
it is perhaps not true
what natsume said

that we come to this world only to die

If This is Us

Claire Donohue Roof

There is the reunionjoy as the lightning brilliant displays its raindespair.
We are in the dreamtime now of riverrushes down the Arizona swimminghole.
Yet, the trees burn also across the hills where temperatures rise as spiritheat.
Refugees from polar icecaps melting into the bluegreen oceans mourn their losses.

Fish swim in the Florida suburb lawns. Superstorms are underestimated by the Weather Channel.
New Jersey loses the beach sands as moontides erode the shores.
Coral reefs stop their breathing, cease their livinghopes of continuous colors.
Tornadoes in their alleys arrive with supercells of whirlingdoom.

We live in the changes. We remember fruit orchards during their harvestmoons.
There are the futurescapes. Fire and ice. Cityscapes scramble for secondchance air.
There is longing for another planet to steal away to now.
This gossamerbreath of my grandson keeps me here on this earth for now.

STRAWBERRY LEDGE FOREVER

Beate Sigriddaughter

Perhaps you remember the story. Vaguely.
Who would hear my voice among the angels
as I cried my fear into the world? Here
I am. Help. Rescue me. I must get out. I must
still praise the strawberry in front of me.

I really should call out its sweetness,
but my voice is hoarse from crying for help.

I hear the waters of oblivion below, white, wild.
I smell the foul breath of the tiger of misogyny above,
and my own scent of fear on this very thin ledge
with the ripe strawberry before me (not to mention
sunset in the making and a thousand stars
waiting their turn as dusk birds flit by).

Do I save my breath for praise or do I cry for help
again? Were I an angel, or God, I would
turn down the volume. Too much noise with all
these laments, these prayerful appeals, inflamed
with hope.

Below the roaring water of oblivion, seductive.
Above the steady pacing tiger.

If I jumped, I would become one with water.
If I climbed, I would become part of the tiger.
When all I want to do is live my tiny moment
of identity, the strawberry optional.

Hear me. I am a poet on a ledge with license
to bend even your legends. In the original
reality, there's merely a second tiger below.
No water. The lady's mouth pronounces
the strawberry sweet.
I am exhausted with reality.

LEAVE

Joannie Stangeland

Daniel has gone so far
away my letters come
back stamped *not picked up,*
the failure of the mail
like that promise printed
on a twenty, in God
we trust, the U.S.A.
and a god I do not

always, my son's future
an extension ladder
leaning three feet below
the one open window
when the house is burning
and he dreams Icarus
falling down his arm—flames
in ink. I change that story—

the boy still in the air
real as a bird, with wings
to feather a mattress,
a pillow, his mother
melting wax into bowls,
wicks lit, stars ablaze
on a night without stars.
I light charcoal out back,

use old news for tinder,
smoke like pigeons winging
east, lighter than paper—
maybe they bring answers,
my words measured with spoons
and cups, a cake I'd make
if he ate cake. Sometimes
they crumble in my throat.

I've saved the handwritten
notes he wrote from boot camp.
At the end of his first
leave I kept the front porch
light on like a candle
in the window, leaning
on that light's gold shoulders
an hour past the door

closing in case he dashed
back home for one more thing
before catching the plane.
A pilot once told me
it's hard to miss the sky,
and each time my son leaves,
he's wearing in this life
like a pair of new boots

or the leather jacket
that had been his father's,
part of me caught, staring
through the front door's smudged glass,
and part of me marching
toward trusting I will learn
again the boy the man
was, and that way know him.

The Last Train Leaves The Station

Tim Suermondt

But we're not on it—

we're not going where it's going anymore.

We might be here out of habit, a last nostalgia

perhaps, a goodbye to all this and that.

Let's begin our adventure arm-in-arm, forget

the calendars—the days are young, enough,

the path a mystery like the Monastery of Archangels,

a light in the distance more hopeful than feared,

your colorful blouses hugging our books in the suitcase.

CORRESPONDENCE FROM A DIFFERENT WAR

Susan Tepper

sweep dead starlings from the deck
every species deserves respect
dot dash

whether native born or
carried in as cargo undetected
dot dash

want me till I burn
you know that feeling going down
dot dash

a type of influenza
not covered in my contract
dot dash

jade beads bought on the street
China 1980
dot dash

that month their gates flung
open to the world
dot dash

Shangai was the low city
known back then
dot dash

bitter January
no skyline to speak of
dot dash

they paid me to hold
all the passports
dot dash

responsible for the tourists
health and well being
dot dash

public spitting in the streets
after dark it was freezing
dot dash

a flick of his eyelid then
nothing much
dot dash

repeat bought them in China
1980 on the street
dot dash

hanging in the vendor carts
off thin wooden tightropes
dot dash

busloads of tourists getting
sick in droves
dot dash

pillowcases marked with red
crosses hung from the sick-bus
dot dash

I know how to buy
off the street
dot dash

to haggle for goods is
an art form
dot dash

do you know the symbol
for double happiness
dot dash

it's Chinese for love
and marriage
dot dash

he mentions the jades being
nothing special in color
dot dash

can't say how pretty they look
following the soft curve of my neck
dot dash.

The Dining Hall

Jon Tribble

for Aretha Montgomery Holmes (1903-1986)

Thursdays we baked bread,
her thin dark fingers
kneading the white dough.
I sat on the wooden stool
watching yellow blocks
of butter melt, calling out
if they started to bubble
and burn on the sides
of the sauce pan. Tubs
of green beans, spinach,
or black-eyed peas stewed—
whole onions floating
in them—while the oven's
meatloaf spiced the air.

But mostly there was bread;
forty or fifty loaves
to feed hungry children
from Granite Mountain
bused in to see the pines
and lake for a week.
Before I left each day
I counted the loaves
to make sure there
was plenty of bread.
Sometimes I forgot,
but we never ran out.

Late spring I'd sneak back
in the woods, eat black-
berries, stalk rabbits,
investigate quail nests,
until I heard her call
from the kitchen door.
I'd run to the last tree

walk out from behind it
hands on my hips, saying,
You can't boss me.
You're not my mother.

The dining hall roared
during meals with chatter
from campers, huge fans
pulling out the heat.
The hair on my legs
stood up when she
opened the oven door
and I'd add another six
to our count. She would cut
a thick heel and brush it
with butter. I'd eat quickly,
palm open below my mouth
to catch every crumb.

HOLOGRAMS

Pamela Uschuk

for Patricia Spears Jones

This is desert's finest season, season of California poppies sunset yellow
and holding up cups of blood orange light
next to penstemon's Elizabeth Taylor lipstick blooms, translucent
waxy pink aloe, stunted lupine singing the blues,
greasewood's yellow flowers verdins consume,
month of mating butterflies and white-winged doves, month
of new desert hares and bobcat kits mewling in our neighbor's eaves, month
before heat's warriors run amok and fires eat the trees, month of Syrian
mothers wiping blood from their babies' mouths, month of political screams
giving birth to racist fists, threats of hunger world-wide, melting ice caps,
month of coal-fired power plants doubling sulfuric smoke, while we survive
hallucinatory as the future etched on a computer screen.

Ambition, Late Life

Helen Wickes

I could say to write another poem I like,
could say to have more years to read poems
I love to read poems I've not yet read
for the first time, to find that picture
of my mother I seem to have lost, to not
call out the idiot a few doors down, how
about to get on the horse, have a good canter,
also to be kind this minute, the next as well,
maybe wake up wanting to be alive, to make
a better Bolognese, a better Genovese, to not
always snarl at the nasty bitch across the street,
and give thanks for the endless streams
of kindness that flow to and around me,
whether I've earned them or not.

Sonnet: Black and White Octaves

Martin Willitts, Jr.

The far birds are musical notes in the sky.
I try to focus them in with a view finder.
The red-orange marigold maintains its color
in black and white photographs. I am trying
to capture the disappearing before they vanish.
These half-tones are a part; the scattered music
becoming raindrops, are another. The orange
color appears, developed among greyscale.

A neighbor trims with a weed-whacker, grass rains.
The machine buzzes like mosquitos, at a high,
whiney-pitch, two octaves above high C.
She squares off the grass, yanks vine weed,
remakes the red-yellow snapdragons. I take photos.
Her hot-pink shorts and blue blouse emerge gray.

HER WISH

Kath Abela Wilson

At the foot of the stairs
the stones lay in wait.
At first,
she felt the heaviness of their silence.
She held her tongue,
and wished to hear a voice.

Later, she began to carry them home.
They gradually took over her house—
from all the ledges and shelves
they stared down at her,
with their indecipherable markings.
She was charmed,
and wished to understand.

Her third wish came true
when she began to eat them,
one by one.
Luckily, the first was small and light—
and it was when it cracked between her teeth,
that she began to hear them speak.

Self Inventory

Bill Yarrow

Sleep like a bear grabs you and won't let go.
Hunger is an ever-opening wound,
brashness a rash whose sudden appearance
is mysterious and unnerving. Like
a long film dissolve, your dreams linger in
wild, new schemes. Your intelligence feels like
a weapon that's been fired in battle
but never been cleaned. Now regret, like a
bus backfire at 3 AM, has startled
you out of your chair. Generosity,
like a foreign city you always meant
to visit, stares at you with pleading eyes.
You're ashamed of selfishness, that blanket
whose softness and warmth you cannot give up.
Tolerance: dollars in someone else's
wallet. Arrogance: cake in the mouth of
a man too old to still be eating cake.
Life, like a kite string, is slipping out of
your hands. But is *any* of this true? No.
Poems are not made of nothing but the truth.

SHOWCASE

Tishani Doshi:
Time, Rhythm & the Luxury of Slowness

by Lark Vernon Timmons

Author, poet, journalist, and dancer Tishani Doshi explores intellect and emotion, light and dark, movement and stillness in her stunning books. Readers experience her poetry as rich in color, rhythm and sensuous images, as in this excerpt from "Monsoon Poem:"

"Because this is a monsoon poem
expect to find the words jasmine,
palmyra, Kuruntokai, red; mangoes
in reference to trees or breasts; paddy
fields, peacocks, Kurinji flowers,
flutes; lotus buds guarding love's
furtive routes. Expect to hear a lot
about erotic consummation inferred
by laburnum gyrations and bamboo
syncopations. Listen to the racket
of wide-mouthed frogs and bent-
legged prawns going about their
business of mating while rain falls
and falls on tiled roofs and verandas,
courtyards, pagodas. Because such
a big part of you seeks to understand

this kind of rain—so unlike your cold
rain, austere rain, get-me-the-hell-
out-of-here rain."

(July/August 2017 issue of *Poetry*)

Born of Welsh-Gujarati parents in 1975, Tishani's epiphany that "there's nothing you cannot do in a poem" hit when she was an undergrad at Queen's University in Charlotte, North Carolina. She was reading Mark Doty, Mary Oliver, James Tate—voices her 19-year-old self experienced as assured, bold and current—voices that "entered her skin and set up tents."

Here, she captures the innocence of youth and sibling connection:

Aj, Age 15

I once chased my brother
Down to the edge of the sea.
We ran past sheets and towels
Spread like sky on the beach,
Between strips of cloth,
Drying chilli and tamarind.
Past slums shackled to the shore—
A maze of thatch roofs and cowdung
Caked walls. And then I lost him,
Searched loudly for him, called his name.
Said, Come out or else—
All the usual tricks.

A woman cleaning rice on her knees
In a blouse done up with safety pins
Pointed to a hut with a single weary finger—
Where he was hiding with a water buffalo.
The low blue lights of the television flickering.
He was inside, laughing so hard,
Shaking his head back and forth,
I thought the joy would come tearing out from him.
Afterwards, we sat in something like silence—
His rare chubby hand in mine,
Listening to the breath of living water.

(Published in *Countries of the Body*, 2006)

Chance Encounter

After earning a master's degree in the Writing Seminars at Johns Hopkins University in Baltimore, Doshi relocated to London in 1999, becoming assistant to the advertising departments of *Harper's* and *Queen* magazines.

In 2001, at 26, a chance encounter with the renowned choreographer Chandralekha led to an unexpected and more serious career in dance. "It was one of those moments," recalls Doshi, "when you hear wheels rattling beneath you, moving you in a direction you had not expected to travel."

> You know her image, the white hair, the intense eyes, the laugh. She lived in a house of swings, facing the Bay of Bengal, in a garden choked with neem trees. The first time I met her she made me do backbends in her living room, inspecting me as though I were a svelte Arabian pony, when in fact I was more like an overfed llama — energetic and agile but with little understanding of a centre. She asked: "Would you like to come work with me?" I said, yes.

Inhabiting the Space of Loneliness

For a decade and a half, Doshi graced stages across the world in Tokyo, Taiwan, Champaner, Bhopal, Bombay, Munich, Calcutta, Toronto, Frankfurt, Salzburg, Sydney, and Madras as lead dancer in Chandralekha's renowned choreography, *Sharira*, which in Sanskrit means "the unending body."

> "Always walk alone," Chandra once told me. We were on a train to Baroda in 2002 for my first performance. Our journey was delayed by 33 hours, and she told me of her travels in Greece and Egypt. How she wandered the streets looking for the Fisher Boy of Thebes, how disappointed she was that the descendants of Ramses had none of the rectangular glory of their ancestors. She talked of postures, of women — how in India they had been carrying water on their hips and putting flowers in one another's hair in the same fashion for centuries. She spoke of the girl of Mohenjo-Daro and herself and me as though we were all part of an unbroken line and could always communicate with one another.

Doshi maintains that writing and talking about dance strips it of its vitality. Here, I believe her imagery belies that notion:

> Everything changes in the dark. Your body, that you imagined you knew so well, becomes a stranger. Arms and legs quiver. You, who have spent so many hours on a stone floor, repeating movements, are no longer you. The first wash of light. Momentary warmth. Tanpuras start, and their stirring drags something up inside you as well. Movement begins from your navel, which is pinned to that small cross on the floor. This is your centre. Over the course of an hour, you will try to hold that centre. You will try to hold time. Many things will vie for your distraction. Bangles clinking softly. Throats being evacuated. The morning's sadness.

"The remarkable thing is that while writers must endure this solitude alone, dancers can share their solitudes."

Doshi elaborates:

> The poet, Marianne Moore, said that the only cure for loneliness is solitude. I think, perhaps, what she meant is that we must learn to inhabit this space of loneliness so that we may know ourselves better, so that we may create. When Shaji leaps on stage at minute 22, the pattern of my breathing changes. It's not just that the anxiety of being alone on stage passes, it is simply that we can be alone together.

Sharira would be Chandralekha's final choreography. Some have questioned whether it is even dance. Its unhurried 63 minute exploration of the essence and power of female sexuality demanded audiences' complete attention and left them mesmerized.

On Dance and Discipline

Doshi trained with the legendary Chandralehka for five years before the choreographer's passing in 2006 and performed another ten years without her. She says, "When Chandra was alive she was always able to make some subtle changes as she observed my body; she knew my body and I danced trusting her gaze." In her absence, Doshi and her partner continued to work on the piece "because in the rehearsal, and especially in the performance of *Sharira*, she [was] present."

"I'd never imposed a discipline on myself before, other than creating a space in which to write," reflects Tishani. "With Chandra you placed a demand on your body which seeped into the work.... I thought, I'm going to change the way I live; writing is going to be my art, and nothing else is important like this is important."

"To have dance in that time was a real anchor," says Doshi, who had spent a decade engaged with poetry without knowing if it would go anywhere. "I felt that even if I never published anything, I was still a dancer and would never give up on poetry, but it mattered less that things weren't happening at a speed that I might have desired."

"You can say that dance taught me to be patient."

Doshi's debut poetry collection, *Countries of the Body*, (Aark Arts Publishing, 2006), won the prestigious Forward Prize for Best First Collection. In these few short lines, she conveys the mood of uncertainty in a time of waiting:

In truth
isn't it a waiting
that never ends

like the chasm between
the cycles of the world
Between separation

and union
longing and abandonment
And somewhere

between the waning
isn't this what
we're left with

the music
of uncertainty
the aftertaste of rain

(Excerpt, "Ode to Drowning", From *Everything Begins Elsewhere*, 2013)

Following Doshi's well-received initial collection, six titles followed, including her first novel, *The Pleasure Seekers* (Bloomsbury Publishing, 2010), which was shortlisted for the Hindu Literary Prize and long-listed for the Orange Prize and the International IMPAC Dublin Literary Award. Her timely and eloquent poem, "Immigrant's Song," is a fine example of her award-winning poetry:

> Let us not speak of those days
> when coffee beans filled the morning
> with hope, when our mothers' headscarves
> hung like white flags on washing lines.
> Let us not speak of the long arms of sky
> that used to cradle us at dusk.
> And the baobabs – let us not trace
> the shape of their leaves in our dreams,
> or yearn for the noise of those nameless birds
> that sang and died in the church's eaves.
> Let us not speak of men,
> stolen from their beds at night.
> Let us not say the word disappeared.
> Let us not remember the first smell of rain:
> It will only make us nostalgic for childhood.
> Instead, let us speak of our lives now —
> the gates and bridges and stores.
> And when we break bread
> in cafes and at kitchen tables
> with our new brothers,
> let us not burden them with stories
> of war or abandonment.
> Let us not name our old friends
> who are unravelling like fairytales
> in the forests of the dead.
> Naming them will not bring them back.
> Let us stay here, and wait for the future
> to arrive, for grandchildren to speak
> in forked tongues about the country
> we once came from.
> Tell us about it, they might ask.
> And you might consider telling them
> of the sky and the coffee beans,

> the small white houses and dusty streets.
> You might set your memory afloat
> like a paper boat down a river.
> You might pray that the paper
> whispers your stories to the water,
> that the water sings it to the trees,
> that the trees howl and howl
> it to the leaves. If you keep still
> and do not speak, you might hear
> your whole life fill the world
> until the wind is the only word.

(Published in *Conflict & Instability*, Axon, 2008)

In her poignant 2017 tribute on the 11th anniversary of Chandralehka's passing, Doshi reflected on things the esteemed choreographer had said about resisting the mechanical and the luxury of slowness:

> But it was loneliness I kept returning to. As a writer I suffer that loneliness because the relationship between the page and the world is a delayed one and not necessarily tangible. But as a dancer, I know loneliness to be a strength. It is like the concept of zero or *shunya*—nothingness and fullness. It's how I assess my limitations and possibilities. On the dark stage I understand that within the body there are multiplicities; that in the rarest of moments I can be the light and the music, the rain on the pavement outside, a prehistoric beating heart.

Language is Landscape

Doshi speaks of living most of her life in and around Madras, which she sees as "the nucleus and the prism" of her vision. "Travel allows an easy alteration of that vision", she says, "but also the necessary displacement that is crucial to epiphany and understanding and, of course, geography plays a part in poetry."

> *"I'm quite tied to the city of my birth, so I've become reliant now*
> *on the cycle of leaving and returning as a way of ensuring*
> *I can still see it, and myself."*

She and her husband live on a remote beach in Tamil Nadu between two fishing villages where in the last 15 years the coast has seen a tsunami, cyclones, floods, and an oil spill.

> The cost of living is cheap, the air is clean, and as writers we can handle the isolation. We constantly talk about growing our own vegetables, getting a cow and installing solar panels, and, while we aren't living off the land yet, we are far removed from urban India. We receive no post, have no television, must sit on a particular part of the bed to get 3G, and leave the compound only when we run out of food.

In recent months, Doshi captivated audiences at literary festivals across India, including Mumbai, Jaipur, and Bengaluru with her riveting showcase of verse and dance drawn from her latest collection.

> For years people asked me about combining dance and poetry. And I always felt that they fed into each other in any case, of course, because of time and rhythm and slowness; and what it means to walk onto a dark stage; and what it means to stare at the blank page; and what it means to give yourself as an artist—in terms of vulnerability. But I never actually felt like I needed to twin the two things in a concrete way until *Girls Are Coming Out of the Woods* (Copper Canyon Press, 2018).

The title poem, "Girls Are Coming Out of the Woods," follows:

> Girls are coming out of the woods,
> wrapped in cloaks and hoods,
> carrying iron bars and candles
> and a multitude of scars, collected
> on acres of premature grass and city
> buses, in temples and bars. Girls
> are coming out of the woods
> with panties tied around their lips,
> making such a noise, it's impossible
> to hear. Is the world speaking too?
> Is it really asking, *What does it mean
> to give someone a proper resting?* Girls are

coming out of the woods, lifting
their broken legs high, leaking secrets
from unfastened thighs, all the lies
whispered by strangers and swimming
coaches, and uncles, especially uncles,
who said spreading would be light
and easy, who put bullets in their chests
and fed their pretty faces to fire,
who sucked the mud clean
off their ribs, and decorated
their coffins with brier. Girls are coming
out of the woods, clearing the ground
to scatter their stories. Even those girls
found naked in ditches and wells,
those forgotten in neglected attics,
and buried in river beds like sediments
from a different century. They've crawled
their way out from behind curtains
of childhood, the silver-pink weight
of their bodies pushing against water,
against the sad, feathered tarnish
of remembrance. Girls are coming out
of the woods the way birds arrive
at morning windows – pecking
and humming, until all you can hear
is the smash of their miniscule hearts
against glass, the bright desperation
of sound – bashing, disappearing.
Girls are coming out of the woods.
They're coming. They're coming.

(Published in *Girls Are Coming Out of the Woods*, 2018)

"Dear Reader"

Doshi's fresh, passionate voice and instinct for reaching deep into the human heart won her a steadily growing legion of fans. Her poems are not only immersive, but often transformative—all fiercely original, richly layered, and authentic:

This body, meagre as it is,
has lost so many limbs to wars, so many
eyes and hearts to romance. But love me,
and I will follow you everywhere—
to the dusty corners of childhood,
to every downfall and resurrection.
Till your skin becomes my skin.
Let us be twins, our blood
thumping after each other
like thunder and lightning.
And when you put your soft head
down to rest, dear Reader,
I promise to always be there,
humming in the dungeons
of your auditory canals—
an immortal mosquito,
hastening you towards fury,
towards incandescence.

(Excerpt from "Contract," from *Girls Are Coming Out of the Woods*, 2018)

"Perhaps to write is a way of not forgetting. Or perhaps it's more than that— an affirmation of the most basic kind. That you once lived in this world; that you experienced joy, desire, betrayal, redemption."

My sincere thanks to Doshi for her time, talent, and kind permissions.

In Conversation with Tishani Doshi

Interviewed by Ami Kaye

Tell me what fascinates you the most about India? Did any of your family members recount stories from ancient mythology and teach you family traditions when you were a child?

Part of the reason I'm a writer is because I wasn't raised on a daily diet of mythology and stories. I yearned for the kind of grandparent at whose knee I could sit, but three of my grandparents died when I was quite young, and the remaining one was more interested in knowing whether I'd learned to make chappathis. Also, no one in my family seemed to think their stories were remarkable enough to speak about, but the few stories I've managed to extract show a remarkable propensity for adventure, persistence, bravery, steadfastness. So, I think I made up a lot of stories in order to make my own mythology. What fascinates me most about India has more to do with the fact that no other country does life and death like she does.

A dual background often yields a unique perspective on life. How did your Welsh heritage contribute to shaping you as a person and writer?

I sometimes pick up my mother's battered red English-Welsh dictionary and pick my way through the words trying to make sense of them. The Welsh is the unknown part of me, the part of me that allows me to move through the world as though I were from anywhere/elsewhere. I have a dream of spending a year at the foot of Mt Snowdon in a cottage, because there's a part of me that wants to belong to Wales, even though I know I don't. To be estranged from your "heritage" is to be confused to some degree, but this confusion leads to all kinds of delicious perspectives—mostly, that boundaries are a fallacy. Belonging—particularly along the lines of nations, ethnicities, religions—is also not as wholesome as it sounds. As a child this was disorienting, but that disorientation eventually widens the world.

You have written about your dance teacher and choreographer, Chandralekha. How have her teachings influenced the way you think and feel about life and art? Have you ever thought of writing about dance?

> I was 26 when I met Chandralekha in Madras, the same age Rilke was when he met Rodin in Paris. And I was perhaps as morose as Rilke was because I just couldn't get enough of *The Notebooks of Malte Laurids Brigge* all the loneliness of Paris, all the sadness of hospitals…. And I suppose, I felt too that what I needed most was to believe that life was finally going to begin. Chandra was a key figure in that transformation. She was the one who broke down the Sanskrit gu-ru for me, as one who removes the darkness. She refused to separate life and art. Her house was a few feet away from the theatre and as a student I learned as much in her room of swings at her informal evening salons as I did in the theatre. I've written several essays about dance but I hope to write something more involved.

We heard you recently attended the Jaipur Literary Festival. Can you share some of your impressions and experiences with us?

> Jaipur is a riot, a carnival for bibliophiles. I've been going there almost every year since 2007, and I've seen it grow from an intimate literary gathering into this outpouring. It's exotic (even for an Indian). I mean, you go to a party in Amber Fort and the voices of Manganiyars are soaring from the fort walls, there are paper lanterns with lights floating in the sky, Paul Beatty is gaping it all just like the rest of us, and you think, yes, this beats cheese and pineapple on a stick. It's so rare for writers to feel that level of grandness in terms of audience and treatment.

As a poetry editor who constantly reads submissions I subconsciously critique and edit, but when I encounter a truly remarkable poem, I find myself jumping in, curious and delighted, not in any hurry to leave and completely consumed. Which poems/poets have done that for you?

> Different poets enter and exit at different times. Some enter and never leave. Ginsberg, for instance, really worked in my early 20s and I can't return to him. Rimbaud was a serious early crush and I could, but haven't returned. Kamala Das was instrumental in opening the

door to poetry and she's always wafting through. AK Ramanujan and his translations, when I found him, were life breath. Elizabeth Bishop was a cold start but is seriously staying put. Emily Dickinson is calling for more serious attentions than I have given. It goes on.

I understand you have traveled widely but of the cities/countries yet to visit, which place calls to you the most?

I have a list: Iran, Burma, South Africa, and then a longer list of secondary and tertiary candidates.

How did your American education/experience inform your writing and worldview?

Two things: how to fend for yourself and the idea that choice is limitless, therefore should you decide to commit your life to the uncertain path of poetry—go for it. It also allowed for the crucial backward glance in terms of viewing India and reconfiguring that new relationship as the person who returns. I think those years in America were some of my loneliest but also where I made genuine friendships and discovered what I wanted to do.

Writing in the digital age carries its headaches and perks. How has technology influenced your communication with fans and other readers and writers? How do you decompress when the "world is too much with you?"

Some years ago I moved from the city down the coast into a pretty rural coastal context where I don't get a newspaper, don't have a TV, and have limited internet. I was hoping to disconnect because I found the constant bombardment of the news overwhelming. Strangely, while I've somewhat insulated myself, I find my work going more and more towards those concerns and bombardments, and social media and technology has been the bridge for that. There is no option of not hearing now. It gives you a headache and the noise is never ending, but perhaps we need to figure out ways of negotiating that noise rather than just shut it off completely. If it all gets too much, I switch into airplane mode and head to the beach with a book.

The poetry circles have seen a lot of heated debate on the popularity of instapoet sensations such as Rupi Kaur. How do you feel about the convergence of pop culture and poetry, and is it necessarily a negative if more young people are developing an interest in poetry through social media influencers?

I'm conflicted, is the truth. I don't think snobbery in art helps anything or anyone, because by undermining a genre you're undermining the emotion where it's coming from and the people who respond to that emotion. But I do have issues with the neatness of instapoetry. Personally, I'm drawn towards poetry that surprises, that challenges language, that is making me see what I don't already see. So there's a certain vision of the poet that I'm interested in. The great leveling of the internet means that we are all poets. Rupi Kaur exists side by side with Bob Hicok. I know whose reading I'd prefer to go to but I also know I'm in a minority.

In your recent poetry collection, *Girls Are Coming Out of the Woods* you tackle powerful themes. It is a timely book, especially against the backdrop of the #MeToo movement. Can you trace the inner journey of this book with us?

I had an earlier poem called *The River of Girls*, where I imagine all India's aborted female fetuses, gathering force like a subterranean river and emerging, fully grown, astride tigers, "their breasts held high like weapons to the sky." This is not a new theme for me. Reclamation is key to poetry. When Jyoti Singh was raped on that Delhi bus in December 2012, I felt there was a radical shift in the way we began to talk about gender violence in India—protests in the streets, changes in legislature. Some months later I was travelling through Ireland by bus, passing these tremendous forests, and I had a vision of armies of girls and women storming out of those woods, with panties around their lips and iron bars in their hands, carrying all their mutilations and scars, but chanting this battle cry. *Girls Are Coming Out of the Woods* began there for me. It's rare that a poem's gestation matches the zeitgeist. I don't think the theme is going to go anywhere any time soon, because the violence certainly hasn't abated, but post #MeToo there has been a realization that even the most powerful can fall, and the girls are coming....

Reviews

BLUE HONEY
by Beth Copeland

Reviewed by Elizabeth Nichols

Beth Copeland's *Blue Honey* is a collection of poetry that lingers in the minds of readers like a gilded memento mori. In fact, Copeland's collection brings to mind the myth of Victorian lachrymatory bottles. Victorian lachrymatory bottles, the myth purports, were used to catch the tears of the mourning. The mourner would then wear black for as long as the tears remained in the lachrymatory bottle, and then end her period of mourning when all the tears evaporated. In reality, these lachrymatory bottles were mere perfume bottles, but the myth of the Victorian tear-catchers remains, echoing in the dark chamber of morbidly fascinating Victorian death ephemera. The myth of the lachrymatory bottle lingers precisely because death ephemera are so alien to twenty-first century society. Copeland, however, does not shy away from death, and instead confronts grief head-on, using modern symbols and imagery as her own memento mori—as vehicles to understand death and, ultimately, to try and come to terms with the loss of loved ones.

In the poem "Sign: *SLOW*," Copeland uses the modern symbol of the traffic sign to approach the subject of death. Playing on the saying that "death stops you in your tracks" Copeland's poem illustrates that the agonizingly slow speed with which serious illness brings about death is itself a road filled pain and indignity. The speaker in "Sign: *SLOW*" spills her grief-fueled anger on the page, imaging herself obliged to drive slowly past the farmhouse of her childhood, watching her father and mother waste away. The speaker rejects the speed forced upon her and her parents and instead speeds past the farmhouse, trying to spare her parents the torturous indignity of a slow death. But, critically, the speaker asks the reader to forgive her for speeding past the farmhouse, as if deep down the speaker knows she is not sparing her parents indignity so much as she is sparing herself pain. "Sign: *SLOW*" captures the torment of the slow death of a loved one by using the modern symbol of a traffic sign in a poem-length conceit, or extended metaphor, to demonstrate that the prolonged death of a loved one is as much a torture for the ailing as it is for the caregiver.

Sign: *SLOW*

Death in the Family. How will slowing
help the people in the white
clapboard farmhouse grieve, of Daddy,

unable to eat solid food, a line
of drool dangling from his lip? Will

a lighter touch on the pedal ease
Mother's journey, hospitalized
with a broken hip, unable to recollect her best

friend's name when I pass the phone? I want
to spare my vanishing

parents the indignity of lingering, so
please forgive me if I burn
rubber past the farmhouse.

Another modern symbol that Copeland uses to great effect is the pearl. Pearls appear in the poems "There," "Onions," and "Fallen Pearls." In "There" Copeland uses the image of a snapped string of pearls to describe her mother's deteriorating mental state. It is a masterful use of imagery that is stunning in its impact. Moreover, jarring the impact of the image is bolstered by the use of short, staccato lines and small stanzas: "Snapped string, pearls scattered. / For her, each / synapse is a pearl, unstrung. Always / surprised, she's / happy as if / I arrived in a blink—a moment / lapsed, finding the lost / bead of my story newly / spun, an orient / orb from the ocean floor." Next, in "Onions," Copeland recalls the way her mother "chopped uncut bulbs like shrunken skulls / dug from the dirt," inserting even in an every-day garden scene a morbid simile. Copeland juxtaposes the layers of the onion with the layers of her own grief, and as the layers are pulled away she reaches "the pearl / white bud at the core / where the girl within / weeps." Like her mother's synapses of pearl, the pearl at the heart of Copeland's layers of grief contains the very center of her self. Finally, in "Fallen Pearls," a string of pearls stands for a string of memories, capturing in one symbol a lifetime of moments shared with Copeland's mother:

> From "Fallen Pearls"
>
> …
>
> …This fragile thread
> binds them into a moment
>
> forgotten but still connected
> somewhere beyond winged
>
> oysters and memories,
> realigned.

Finally, Copeland's titular modern symbol of death and grief is blue honey. As the speaker explains in the poem "Sandhills Gold," "How it [the honey] turns / blue or why it only happens / here no one knows. Some / think bees feed on bruised huckleberries, scuppernongs / or kudzu blossoms." The symbol of blue honey transforms something naturally sweet into something strange, much like a Victorian memento mori in the eyes of modern society. Additionally, the color blue is to used to describe a dip in feelings; if one is feeling blue, they're sad. Blue honey, therefore, is a symbol of dichotomy: sweetness and sadness. This bittersweet symbol flavors the speaker's memories as she describes talking "blue honey into blue eyes that / stared back in a blur / of lost memory and sleep." The speaker tries to evoke the sweetness of shared memories around his "bellowing hives," but her sweetness does not find purchase in the haze of her father's dementia. Frustrated, the speaker's grief pours out of her, and she tells the reader,

> …I want this
> grief to dissolve like a lemon
>
> lozenge on my tongue, I want
> to taste the sweetness

of mornings
before sorrow, anger, and remorse

soured my vision of being
young and oblivious to his

pain, I want my words to flow
like a vein

onto the blue-line page as holy
Honey flowed from his white

hives onto our bread, our tongues, our lives.

Blue honey, then, symbolizes what the reader is left with at the passing of her father: sweet memories soured by her grief. It is no wonder, perhaps, that the speaker begs the omniscient narrator to not "let [her] linger / in the ellipses / of dementia and disease / murmuring goodbye again / and again to family and friends." Instead, she asks the omniscient reader to "Write a simple sentence with a period at the end." In other words, the speaker does not want her grief to linger. The speaker wants her period of mourning to end; she wants her tears to dissolve in the lachrymatory bottle of her heart. Copeland's *Blue Honey*, in fact, very well may be the period that the speaker is seeking. With modern symbols as her own memento mori, Copeland's collection wrestles with grief, forcing the reader to confront loss, death, and the human condition.

ILLUSION OF AN OVERWHELM
by John Amen

REVIEWED BY ELIZABETH NICHOLS

John Amen's *Illusion of an Overwhelm* plumbs the depths of the modern soul, exposing the confusion in the juxtaposition of psyche and body, nationalism and identity, and love and loss. Desire runs rampant in Amen's poems, crystalizing in the personification of Anima a la Swiss psychiatrist and psychoanalyst Carl Jung. Amen brings Jung's concept of amina to life by sculpting her with the speaker's own rib; she is the speaker's inner desires, his unconscious writ large. Like Jung's anima, this feminine Anima has both light and dark aspects. Amen's Anima can bring life and development, or cause petrification and death: she is an "illusion" that "keeps giving keeps taking." Here, as in Jung's work, Anima is the speaker's feminine unconscious, "chewing her boredom, / flirting with the clerks." With Anima the speaker, a male subject, is opening up to his emotions and a broader spirituality. Moreover, Anima affords the speaker a psychic sensitivity toward himself and others. By personifying Anima, Amen makes her an independent force throughout *Illusion of an Overwhelm*, ever-present as the speaker acknowledges the nature of his desires, and at times loses control of them. Indeed, Amen's Anima is a feminine force that is both alluring and repulsive, desirable and dangerous. The reader is made to feel that at any time the speaker could be overwhelmed by this powerful, personified Anima, falling into the waking dream of his own unconscious. Together, the speaker and the reader unmoor "from the world [they want] to love, / leaving behind its sharp edges, its legalistic memory" in favor of Anima.

From *Hallelujah Anima*

1

The purpose of desire
is to propagate desire

    & its concomitant recoil:
ambivalence is truth.

Anima works the cattle prod, works the courtiers,
a new breed texting resentment poems
to the hum of an electric choker.

I chased Anima before I even met her,
black clouds gathering over water,
still chase her through labyrinths of ache,
pining for that tropical season when I was heir to a lovesick tune
in these more temperate times
I no longer hear.

A man drags his secrets from dream to dream,
secrets that drag him through a hundred skins.
Anima says give them to me,
but she never takes them,
& I just can't let them go.

    In the second section of his chapbook, Amen takes the reader from the heady vision of the unconscious ruled by Anima to a gutted landscape of American myths. The reader meets J, a man suffering from PTSD that lost his life to suicide. J is one of the central figures in the American myths. His world is controlled by white gods, white fathers, white disembodied mothers, and black sons. J chafes against the white father's world, assuming a stance of rebellion until he can no longer handle life as a black son, a marked outcast: "…A rope's lowered, / *Grab it,* the prop master bellows, but J's off script, / black son on a bare stage, middle finger to the sky." Like J, the speaker is also a black son that turns his back on the myths that white father spouts as truths. The speaker paints his life in small-town America, clipped resentment oozing from each stanza: "I'm the black son; doesn't matter if this is factual, / it's my life story, the metaphor that locks my throat. / Raised in a flooded town, I belly-crawled dirt roads / in a county of Stars & Bars, pale Jesus & pit bulls, / succubi lying open-legged in a hayloft." Amen's portrait of the speaker's world is timely and carries with it a poignant warning:

From *The American Myths*

14

...Don't believe the white
father, his myth of origin; truth is, he turns a crank
in the background, he keeps the keys, he sprays the
fig tree with pesticide when believers aren't looking.
Don't entertain that crap about the dead mother being
sculpted from a rib, bear in mind that this white father
is simply another white father in a line of white fathers,
each of whom burned in a pyre of Jacksons, screwed
by his own ballyhoo.

    Here, the speaker's warning for the reader is uses Christian symbolism to argue against the white father's myths. He alludes that the white father, God/Jesus, is only one in a line of white fathers that try to control people with myth. Moreover, the line of white fathers also stands for the overwhelming majority of white men—white fathers—that hold positions of power in American society. The speaker also tarnishes the white fathers' myths by calling their pyres burning piles of money, exposing their hypocrisy. Amen, in other words, uses his own symbolic figures—white father, disembodied mother, and black son—to reveal the insidious nature of American myths. The myth of the American dream, of wealth through hard work alone, of "IRAs, 401ks, insurance, a world of / pyramids & smoke, prescriptions & proscriptions that might / win you admission to a grand gala that fizzled decades ago." Finally, Amen ends his beautifully biting exposé of American myths by alluding a to America's contemporary political climate:

From *The American Myths*

7

...

Now's his chance to sway public opinion, white
God as his personal Super PAC. The black son
thumbs-up for the camera, toothy on the billboard.
The black son roaring on Super Bowl Sunday.
This is how he storms the world; that's payback,
baby, manifest destiny, that's o bless America.

Amen not only dredges up images at the depths of American myths, but also finds the darker parts of the modern soul in the section entitled *My Gallery Days*. Modernity juts out from Amen's lines with abbreviations, text-speech, and web address symbols: w/, yr, sd, and @. This section of Amen's *Illusion of an Overwhelm* reads like the drug-fueled diary of an anxious 20-something desperately trying to understand himself, the world, and his place in that world. "Ours is the real lost generation," the speaker insists to the reader, "days like vanishing data, / insomniac Superflats inclined to brood, / can a nihilist find her voice in the khaki suburbs?" However, in this haze of modern soul-searching, there is more at risk than just a cringe-worthy blog post. Drugs up the ante of modern soul-searching, making each moment of existential angst a work of art or of sudden death: "A purple hearse idled beside a green ladder: / Bill Casaman's Tompkins Pk funeral. / He nailed his brain on webcam: lo-fi suicide." The speaker recognizes the danger, but cannot seem to pull himself from the torrent, even at the expense of his own creativity: "Louisa smirked, prodded for a vein in her right arm. / I swear in the silence the music inside me was crumbling."

Thankfully, at the end of the chapbook, Amen produces love in *Portrait of Us*, as if the life-threatening existential angst of *My Gallery Days* eases into the light at the end of the tunnel. The form of Amen's poems in *Portrait of Us* flows with long stanzas that descend gracefully to the end of the page with single indents. He experiments with the flow and placement of stanzas as if to capture the pace of a slow, ardor-filled breath. Love is both metaphysical and physical, transporting the speaker from the tangible world into an effervescent, bright dreamscape:

From *Portrait of Us*

3

...

Inside you,
I'm in another world,
deeper in this world,
where two worlds meet.
I wash up on a weedy shoal.
I look around for you,
gathering starfish & broken shells,
the gifts at my disposal,
resume the long stroking movement
through long brooding waters,
to finally fall in love with drowning,
to see it's possible
to love things
just as they are
a woman
just as she is.

Interestingly, the speaker's description of his love recalls the personified Anima from the beginning of *Illusion of an Overwhelm*. With Anima, as with his love, the speaker is in another world: his subconscious. Moreover, the sensation of drowning recalls the image of water in Amen's first poem: "black clouds gathering over the water… / pining for that tropical season / when I was heir to a lovesick tune." Moroever, like Anima, the speaker's love turns out to have a dual nature: she brings the speaker joy as well as sorrow. In the last poem of the collection, the speaker grieves for his lost love. The speaker describes flesh as if he is describing Anima, as "home to the tyrant and the saint," before ultimately ending the story of himself and his lover as a dissolution of a moment: "the birth & dispersion of light and matter." With this language, Amen returns the reader to the realm of the metaphysical, to the world of Anima. In the end, John Amen's *Illusion of an Overwhelm* pulls the reader through a kaleidoscopic vision of the modern soul, guided by Anima, to meet desire, myth, angst, and love head-on. Amen's poetry, in other words, pulls at the veil of illusion and overwhelms the reader with the beauty of revealed truths.

Imagine: New and Selected Poems
by Shanta Acharya

Reviewed by Andrea Witzke Slot

In a world of single hits (of both the musical and poetic kind), it is refreshing to read the arc of a poet's work and development of talent over a longer period of time. Such is the pleasure gained from reading Shanta Acharya's *Imagine: New and Selected Poems* (HarperCollins, India, 2017), which incorporates poems from five collections spanning the years 1994-2010 alongside a generous selection of new poems. Acharya has lived a life of rich and varied cultural experiences not only of two countries, including her birth country of India and her adopted country of England, but also of varied academic and professional paths. After earning her MA at Ravenshaw College in Cuttack, India, Acharya attended Oxford on a scholarship, followed by time as a Visiting Scholar at Harvard before joining the asset management team of the Morgan Stanley in London in 1985. Acharya has published eleven books in various genres and on wide-ranging subject matter, including finance, literary criticism, fiction, and, of course, poetry. Although we should of course be cautious at equating the poetic "I" with the poet, Acharya's personal experiences thread through the range of ideas and images in *Imagine*, especially as the poems shift in purpose and content over the years. Equally, though, there is a constant in the canvas of Acharya's work: a restless, sometimes somber, sometimes joyful, philosophical exploration of the artist's place in the world.

The book begins with a range of poems from Acharya's first collection *Not This, Not That*. Many of the poems in this section are memories of time and place and parents often explored through extended analogies and metaphors, and often reflective of a child's wide-eyed view of the world as encountered in the vibrant imagery of the poem "Dussehra In Cuttack." But these poems are not simply recollections. They are testament to the young life of an artist, the desire to make something permanent from one's earliest memories, and a restless ambition to fulfill the dream of an artistic life. And yet art is more than its maker, as is suggested in the poem "The Vulnerable Plot of Green:"

> Under our very different sun
> there are no illusions
> about the sacred realm of art,
> the shaping power of the imagination,
> nor for that matter the imperial self.

The dual concerns of artistic destiny and disillusionment become more complex as we move to the poems of Acharya's second collection, *Numbering Our Days' Illusions*. In this section, a fragmented story emerges—a story that is unmistakably sown with pain and heartache. The reader knows the pain is genuine. The reader knows the heartache is real. Perhaps this is what makes these particular poems come to life, as there is emotional urgency unique to this section of *Imagine*. The end-lines of "Honeymoon" address an invisible "you," one who caused suffering, and one who "drank deep the honey / and left me with the cold platter of a moon." These lines are made even more poignant by following on the heels of the troubling "Arranged Marriage." In another short poem, "Resigned," we encounter a different kind of reckoning in the haunting lines "Naked I came / reduced to my alphabets, / a tree trying to be a seedling / confessing all /through shifts in our stances of embracing." And yet as we reach the poem "Meditation in a Bathtub," "the rising steam of illusions" seems to mark the beginning of a meditation on the how pain and illusions might inform a life. These illusions, Acharya's poems suggest, are the very stuff of greater philosophical and human understanding.

In the poems from the collection *Looking In, Looking Out*, the philosophy of Acharya's work expands and intensifies through a number of ekphrastic poems and ideas rooted in art, myth, and nature. In the poem "Snowdrops," the tiny flowers—"[m]essengers of hope, figurines of faith and charity, / fragile creations exuding dignity—" become much more than mere snowdrops as they "bow, emptying themselves of all desire, / make peace with themselves without walking on fire;" while the poem "Survival" pairs playfulness with introspection as it describes the astrological sign of Cancer, a sign that "breeds vulnerable, / tenacious and excitable / crustaceans programmed / to triumph against the odds." The curious creatures of "Survival" are both mischievous and serious, as they don the everyday armor of self-protection:

> Crabs, lobsters, beetles, scarabs,
> snails, turtles, tortoises—

> all self-contained, sensitive creatures—
> supporting their crosses on their backs
> negotiate in an uncertain,
>
> unpredictable, unforgiving world,
> making themselves at home everywhere,
> being eternally prepared.

The next section, which includes work from Acharya's collection *Shringara*, begins with the poems "Highgate Cemetery" and "Loneliness," the latter of which is a meditation on the pain of a lonely life and how that loneliness might carry its own weight of intelligence and understanding: "Discover in loneliness the continents of yourself, / it's a secure place to wander in for nobody can trespass, / unless you let them in. It is an island of freedom and peace." This section includes touching elegies to both a grandfather and a father in which the poet searches for meaning in "the journey of the soul," marking the beginning of a difficult acceptance of the belief that "grief too must enrich us." These poems lead into a wider vision in the poems in the fifth section titled "Dreams that Spell the Light." Here, readers encounter an almost transcendental exploration of time and place in such poems as "Return of the Exile," which opens with such questions as "Where do we go when our time is up, / our insignificant lives / tempered by the questions we ask?"

Sometimes, as with the work in the final section of *Imagine*, Acharya's poems approach complex philosophical subjects in an almost prose-like language. Perhaps because of the scope of the subject matter and the nature of the ideas in these latter poems, I felt they lacked some of the freshness and spontaneity of her earlier work. But then perhaps the subject matter of these poems rises above their poetic forms; indeed, I found myself longing for a larger exploration of Acharya's rich ideas in the rounded lines and sentences of an essay. There are poems throughout the book, too, in which multiple images sometimes dilute the gems of most striking poetic imagery. But the beauty of Acharya's work is less about word-mongering than word and world building. Acharya is a poet who writes poems that are sensual and filled with memories and philosophical musings, poems in which one senses not just a desire but also an absolute *necessity* to write, and thus fulfill the destiny of an artist, one who feels the utmost dedication to her work. In fact the process of writing, Acharya's work suggests, is a source of philosophical reckoning in itself: a never-ceasing exploration of human desires and failings and all that hurts and delights and confounds us in this brief life. There is a tender vulnerability amongst Acharya's poems combined with occasional humor, which reminds us that humans rarely reach the potential of which they are capable, and that this too is an inevitable part of every artist's life.

Within Acharya's *Imagine: New and Selected Poems* we find a range of intense philosophical meditations on the nature of imagination and the artist's place in the world. But, as her work builds its crescendo throughout the years, it becomes much than that. Acharya's poems recreate the arc of an artist's life and a constant desire to find meaning through one's work, even if that desire is accompanied by a kind of whispering fear that each of us is little more than a ghost that haunts the strange watery days of our memories.

KAFKA'S SHADOW
by Judith Skillman

REVIEWED BY LINDA KIM

Subtle and obscured, Judith Skillman's poems in *Kafka's Shadow* fully embody the existential struggle of an artist. Her speculation of Kafka's background makes for poetry that is rich and sly with hidden meanings, imaginings. Enjambment contrasts abruptly with syntax to denote changes in mentality while associations drip ripe with tangible imagery and metaphor. Unexpected, astonishing turns of phrase paint a scene within every poem; every line is a window into Kafka's mind, a lens in which to inform our understanding of everything a poem can do. Such phrasing seems apparent in its simplicity, but there is a complexity underneath, just shy of the reader's gaze.

Lineation is key to narrative. Expectations ebb and flow as Skillman skillfully directs and controls our gaze. The poet examines Kafka's every social interaction, his family connections, lovers and acquaintances. Her narration takes on his perspective, but his persona is viewed from a detached storytelling distance with each piecemeal vignette unfolding with the grandeur of mythology, as if every facet of Kafka's history is to be canonized and studied.

There is allurement and reverence here. Skillman depicts an artist discombobulated by the human condition, disconcerted with his state of existence. Heavy is the revelation that lands on Kafka's crown, who broods and obsesses over every narrative development—he who is both puppet and muse. To be human is to be weighed down by loneliness. Every being is inherently alone. Kafka's belief in this unshakeable inevitability, this finality, encapsulates his nihilism. Kafka's detachment barely holds back the threatening realities that are nightmarish and enigmatic in tone.

Wretchedly overcome with the frustrations of being an artist, Kafka is left adrift under the yoke of familial expectations. We become as subsumed by his daily mundanity as he is:

> I used to like to walk
> downstairs into the world. There a family
>
> ate and drank. My sisters' cheekbones high,
> their eyes bright and well slept. I was punished
>
> for not being an entrepreneur—for
> wanting to write.

Always Kafka holds himself at a distance. He only reluctantly associates himself with "a family," thus divorcing himself from reality, because he rejects it in favor of his own. He escapes into words. Otherwise, Kafka would be constantly under attack by a passionless family and an indifferent society, both of which see little worth in his scribblings. It is dissociation at its best.

What kind of environment could have possibly produced Kafka? It is fascinating to stare at the wreckage. Starvation is a hunger that transcends beyond mundane physicality. When she depicts the ambition and hunger lurking in Kafka, Skillman remarks about the state of artistry itself. Her complexity of meaning, store within brevity and subtextual meanderings, represent a metaphysical starvation for passion. The act of creation is Kafka's own means of escape, his imagination the only retreat from a too-harsh world. He is consumed by the passion of labor: "The stories waited to be born. Labor / after labor between bouts of illness. / I ask my awful god for an appetite!"

If so, then Kafka's muse is a cruel and capricious god. How much despair does it take to fuel his works? Skillman's empathetic portrayal of his spindly inner workings transforms our own absorption of his seminal works, a metamorphosis of our own. We become Kafka: a tormented genius, Skillman's beloved subject. We become just as helplessly caught up in his manic lusts for creativity and escape as she does. Kafka's understanding of the world is heavily enmeshed in his suffering. Yet the search for balms is constantly thwarted. It is an unending struggle. It is telling that the one source of beauty and respite within the whole book, his mother's beautiful garden, is besieged by "hoarfrost" and death. Kafka can only obsess over endings, her disappearance, and the inevitable dissolution of her marriage:

> Afterwards, when the passion cooled,
> why did she stay with him?
> ...
> Would she disappear from the room,
> the house, and with her the garden
>
> that bloomed under her supervision with lilacs
> for two weeks each spring?
> Only fourteen days, their scent a fresh rose
>
> with a hint of honey, like her feelings,
> meant to be suppressed especially at this,
> the most buoyant point of year.

The idealized nurturer has a purity of purpose, but Kafka's mother is so muted and faded that he is left neglected and starved. Instead, the yearning for an absent mother figure contrasts sharply with an all-powerful and all-consuming "father-monster" figure. When Skillman casts Kafka in the place of Isaac after God demands a sacrifice, she shows the depths of depravity within Kafka's mortal enemy:

> When God cries out—
> "Stop! Hermann, I was only testing your faith!
> Your son is spared, slit the throat of a young ram
> and go home," the older Kafka, his hands
> around Franz's neck, replies, "Too late.
>
> I am far more obedient
> than that clown you took me for—
> the other, named Ibrahim."

The "father-monster," supposedly devout, instead perverts the purpose of religion and corrupts it. His hypocrisy is a mockery of religion, thus reflecting Kafka's deep skepticism in all things God. Hermann, that godlike beastly man, is the single greatest antagonist that looms large throughout the poetry. He is "god incarnate." But Skillman understands that Kafka's loathing for his father is matched only by his self-disgust, a filthiness he can never shake off. And there is a deep anxiety at the center of his thoughts: the terrible conviction that he, too, will turn into his father, a monster. And thus lovers are never sufficient in distraction while his mind only skitters at the thought of propagating children. And even when he does wish for succor, separation will prevent his desire.

The line "He in Prague, she in Berlin, / and Venus rising." not only highlights sharp physical distance, but the finality of the period. And the invocation of Venus here can only allude to the impossibility of being: an abstract and imaginary harmony. After all he is nothing more than an insect, a fell creature, a dung beetle to be swatted aside by caregivers:

> The housecleaner who taunted him
>
> *dung beetle, dung beetle*
> pushes his carcass with her broom.
> She suspects he is gone.
>
> Yes, an accordion without air.
> The little legs quiet,
> an abdomen no longer round.
>
> His death wish fulfilled

A subhuman devoid of humanity, Kafka is stripped of everything wholesome and worthy. Skillman's characterization is astounding. In her hands, he is putty malleable in shape and non-euclidean in form. Kafka sees and processes a skewed reality just as settings reflect his own askew psychology. The more he is immersed in filth, the more Skillman emphasizes the prison of his own making: his psyche. "Bacilli" and disease breed only a tendency to see destruction in living things and a tendency to be drawn towards a self-defeatist irony.

Kafka is obsessed with the poverty of his circumstances, preoccupied with how ridden his home is with filth and dirt and unholy things. "Here and there yellows turn brown, rust / as if with illness. The doctor has found / no cure for moods." His preoccupation with spiders and other low animals like moles and vermin shows his own existential anxieties, a perpetual dehumanization. In his worldview, even something as innocuous as "Miniature Cakes" cannot be safe:

> Kafka likes their outsides
> wrapped in icing, decorated
> with letters, topped
> with Snow Babies and elves.
> He likes truffles,
> biting through softness.
> An intense pleasure, and then
> the sinking. So it goes
> in rooms without women.
> A city made for fathers,
> fathers, and more fathers.

Kafka's imagination is a stickiness that clings. Settings reflect psychology, and he is at utter odds with himself. There is no safety in his home. He feels unwelcome there. He can only reach for, with grasping fingers, a cyclical despair.

As he battles with himself, Kafka must temper his hopes for respite and peace against a learned cynicism, a history of incessantly dashed dreams. Kafka is beset by the madness of his many nameless afflictions. But Skillman puts words to those afflictions, such as when she says, "Kafka's knife, brought to bear / when his nerves are needled / once more by a threat or a curse, / frayed by depression, / singed by self-deprecation."

In *Kafka's Shadow*, the artist is defined by his own absence, the negative cast of his image, and the frustrations of existence. He is a reduction of shadows. He is the creation of his father, an offspring of neglect, the product of legacy and abuse. And the stronger the father looms large in the poems, the more the son disappears like a wraith.

WHORELIGHT
by Linda Ashok

Reviewed by Linda Kim

Memory is a tapestry upon which Linda Ashok's poems weave and intertwine to tell a story of how the smallest moments in life can end up resonating into the biggest of impacts. In *whorelight* the poet very deliberately understands how freeing the constraints of form can be, how cathartic the relationship between form and words can be on the page. Perception is fluid. Her focus on the flexibility of reality, of the ways in which an individual's experiences can make it bend, shows in the variety in form and a lightness of being:

> Running in the morning light trying to catch the falling tide I
> gather your voice in my shoes and wear them back to
> where I begin writing this poem too shy to confess
> how it notices countries walking naked through your
> face and people too happy to go on a walk with animal
> dreams on their tongues. My feet, wet and luminous.
> My nails, little glass screens offering a preview of the
> undersea, of debris forming new structures.

Poetic associations, beget by a lush imagination, thus coalesce into rich fertile landscapes of imaginings. Such skillful handling of associative thought underpins the whole of her poetry. But water can just as easily be a "laceration of the waves" instead of tranquil.

In Ashok's world, "memory / is biodegradable, / that it blends / with the berries / in the soil, / in the scum / under feet." It is "a nestling / its mother gone." It can be reviewed through the lens of a fractured kaleidoscope, reflecting the speaker's state of mind. Or it can be viewed through a contrasting surrealist images that speak of the deeper anxieties of the mind:

> But I am thirty, just finished paying my debts.
> It is time, you should be a mother, said
> my homemaker girlfriends.
> I look at a fledgling in the nest or a cub
> in the manger, I look at an insect nursing her
> kind or a woman breastfeeding her newborn,
> I feel an ache and the skin on my body
> falls like a garment loosely stitched,
> worn out through inconsiderate rubs.
> The coconut tree too, laughs at me
> showing off her tender water babies.

Ashok's poetry is sensory, sensual, and intimate. Femininity, womanhood, and motherhood are cast against a backdrop of loss while relationships and sex have a vivacity even amidst solemnity.

The natural order of things is revered. It is a fascination that manifests in nature descriptions and motifs such as insects, birds, and woods. Earth and water itself becomes elemental. But nature, when combined with the poet's themes of maternity, underpins the natural world with unsettling implications. In the mind of a childless woman yearning for progeny, something as innocuous as an "empty nest" can become an image of despair. Daily reality becomes rife with self-flagellation. Identity becomes solidified more by the absence of things rather than actuality.

But nature still blooms, illuminated by its own beauty, even in the midst of inevitable decay. When the speaker recalls a dead deer in "When You Talk About A Dead Deer," the act of remembrance is both anguished and revelatory:

> The buds in my garden respond to such grief with a
> refusal to open up their petals in full light. Air, dank
> with sorrow, makes my garden smell like a cemetery.
> Ghosts juggle in the bath under feet and I can only
> hear a trombone, a devastating note grafted by the
> wind on my broken cello still living with a heart and
> two kidneys.

Emotions are rich. All facets of sorrow are explored in Ashok's poetry. Guilt, regret, and grief are mainstays in the emotional landscape of *whorelight*. There is pain in the act of remembering—of lacerating open old wounds—but there is healing, too, in the exposure.

There is still beauty to be found in the imperfection:

> A neckpiece
> of sugared fireflies
> A lighthouse full of wrecks
> A sea wasp
> that obeys touch
> A yarn
> of sinking
> And distance
> that keeps us together

Thus there is a fragility in Ashok's various speakers as they recall their deepest hurts, their most buried emotions. Yet soon the retelling this frailty can be transformed anew into resilience. Once, such fraught feelings could only be repressed. Now they can finally break free and arise.

PUBLICATION CREDITS

Shanta Acharya: "Kabul" was featured in *Imagine: New and Selected Poems by Shanta Acharya* published by HarperCollins Publishers, India, 2017

CONTRIBUTOR NOTES

Shanta Acharya, born and educated in Cuttack, India, won a scholarship to Oxford, and was among the first batch of women admitted to Worcester College in 1979. A recipient of the Violet Vaughan Morgan Fellowship, she was awarded the Doctor of Philosophy for her work on Ralph Waldo Emerson in 1983. She was a Visiting Scholar in the Department of English and American Literature and Languages at Harvard University before joining Morgan Stanley in London in 1985. She has worked in the asset management industry since and has written extensively on the subject. The author of eleven books, her publications range from poetry, literary criticism and fiction to finance. Her latest is *Imagine: New and Selected Poems* (HarperCollins, India; 2017). Founder of Poetry in the House, Shanta hosted a series of monthly poetry readings at Lauderdale House, Highgate, in London from 1996-2015. She has twice served on the board of trustees of The Poetry Society as well as The Poetry School and the Arvon Foundation in the UK.

Sofiul Azam has three poetry collections *Impasse* (2003), *In Love with a Gorgon* (2010), *Safe under Water* (2014) and edited *Short Stories of Selim Morshed* (2009). His poems are published in *Prairie Schooner, Poetry Salzburg Review, The Journal, Orbis, The Cannon's Mouth, Postcolonial Text,* etc. and anthologized in *Journeys, Caught in the Net, Poets Against War, Poetry for Charity Volume 2*. He is now working on *Earth and Windows: New and Selected Poems*. He teaches English at Victoria University of Bangladesh, having taught it before at Independent University Bangladesh, Southeast University and Royal University of Dhaka.

Sofia A. Bening is the first Singaporean recipient of the Keats-Shelley Young Romantics Prize. She enjoys celebrating the weird and dissecting human nature through her writing. She has been published in Singapore in the *All In! Snack Fiction Anthology* by the National Book Council.

Margo Berdeshevsky, born in New York city, often writes and lives in Paris. *Before The Drought*, her newest collection, is from Glass Lyre Press, September 2017. (In an early version, it was finalist for the National Poetry Series.) Berdeshevsky is author as well of *Between Soul & Stone*, and *But a Passage in Wilderness*, (Sheep Meadow Press.) Her book of illustrated stories, *Beautiful Soon Enough*, received the first Ronald Sukenick Innovative Fiction Award for Fiction Collective Two (University of Alabama Press.) Other honors include the Robert H. Winner Award from the Poetry Society of America, a portfolio of her poems in the *Aeolian Harp Anthology* #1 (Glass Lyre Press,) the *& Now Anthology of the Best of Innovative Writing*, and numerous Pushcart Prize nominations. Her works appear in the American journals: *Poetry International, New Letters, Kenyon Review, Plume, The Collagist, Tupelo Quarterly, Gulf Coast, Southern Humanities Review, Pleiades, Prairie Schooner, The American Journal of Poetry*, & *Jacar Press—One*, among many others. In Europe her works have been seen in *The Poetry Review (UK), Levure Littéraire, The Creative Process, The Wolf, Europe, Siècle 21*, & *Confluences Poétiques*. A multi genre novel, *Vagrant*, and a hybrid of poems, *Square Black Key*, wait at the gate. She may be found reading from her books in London, Paris, New York City, or somewhere new in the world. Her *Letters from Paris* may be found in Poetry International, here: http://pionline.wordpress.com/category/letters-from-paris/ For more info kindly see: http://margoberdeshevsky.com

Kirkus Reviews named **Sharon Chmielarz**'s tenth book of poetry, *The Widow's House*, one of 100 Best Indie Books in 2016. Her other recent book, *Visibility: Ten Miles* was a finalist for the Midwest Book Award in poetry and photography. A new book, *Little Eternities*, was published in 2017.

Joan Colby has published widely in journals such as *Poetry, Atlanta Review, South Dakota Review, Gargoyle, Pinyon, Little Patuxent Review, Spillway, Midwestern Gothic* and others. Awards include two Illinois Arts Council Literary Awards and an Illinois Arts Council Fellowship in Literature. She has published 21 books including *Selected Poems* from FutureCycle Press which received the

2013 FutureCycle Prize and *Ribcage* from Glass Lyre Press which has been awarded the 2015 Kithara Book Prize. Three of her poems have been featured on Verse Daily and another is among the winners of the 2016 Atlanta Review International Poetry Contest. Her newest books are *Carnival* from FutureCycle Press, *The Seven Heavenly Virtues* from Kelsay Books and *Her Heartsongs* from Presa Press. Colby is a senior editor of FutureCycle Press and an associate editor of *Good Works Review*. Website: www.joancolby.com. Facebook: Joan Colby. Twitter: poetjm.

Rachel Dacus is the author of *Gods of Water and Air*, a collection of poetry, prose, and drama, and the poetry collections *Earth Lessons* and *Femme au Chapeau*. Her poetry and prose have appeared in *Atlanta Review, Boulevard, Prairie Schooner, The Pedestal,* and *Valparaiso Poetry Review*. *The Renaissance Club*, her time travel novel involving the great Italian sculptor Gianlorenzo Bernini, is forthcoming in January 2018 from Fiery Seas Publishing. Her fourth poetry collection, *Arabesque*, is forthcoming in August 2018 from FutureCycle Press.

Yoko Danno is Japanese. She writes poetry solely in English. Her poems have appeared internationally in many journals and anthologies, online and in print. Her books of poetry include: *Epitaph for memories* (The Bunny and the Crocodile Press, 2002), *The Blue Door* (The Word Works, 2006), *trilogy & Hagoromo: A Celestial Robe* (The Ikuta Press, 2010), *Aquamarine* (Glass Lyre Press, 2014) and *Woman in a Blue Robe*(Isobar Press, 2016). The 2nd edition of her translation, *Songs and Stories of the Kojiki,* a collection of creation myths, songs and historical narratives compiled in the 8th-century Japan, was published by Red Moon Press (2014). URL: http://www.ikutapress.com/danno3.html

Lori Desrosiers' poetry books are *The Philosopher's Daughter* (Salmon Poetry, 2013), a chapbook, *Inner Sky* (Glass Lyre Press 2015) and *Sometimes I Hear the Clock Speak* (Salmon Poetry, 2016). Her work has been nominated for a Pushcart Prize. She edits *Naugatuck River Review*, a journal of narrative poetry. She teaches Literature and Composition at Westfield State University and Holyoke Community College, and Poetry in the Interdisciplinary Studies program for the Lesley University M.F.A. graduate program.

Tishani Doshi, a writer and dancer of Welsh-Gujarati origin, was born in Madras, India in 1975. After studying at Queens College, then later gaining a Masters in the Writing Seminars at Johns Hopkins University, she moved to London in 1999 to become an advertising assistant at *Harper's* and *Queen* magazine. In 2001, she returned to India where she became a dancer with the choreographer Chandralekha. Doshi now also works as a freelance journalist, contributing to various newspapers such as *The Guardian, The International Herald Tribune, The New Indian Express,* and *The National.* Her first book of poetry, *Countries of the Body* (2006), won the Forward Poetry Prize (Best First Collection) in 2006. Her first novel, *The Pleasure Seekers* (2010), became shortlisted for the Hindu Best Fiction Award and longlisted for the Orange Prize for Fiction and the International IMPAC Dublin Literary Award. *Girls Are Coming Out of the Woods* (2017), a collection of poems, is her latest book. Tishani divides her time between a village by the sea in Tamil Nadu and elsewhere.

Lisken Van Pelt Dus was raised in England, the US, and Mexico, and lives in western Massachusetts. She teaches high school and martial arts, and her poetry can be found in many journals. Pudding House Press published her chapbook, *Everywhere at Once,* in 2009, and a full-length book, *What We're Made Of,* was released by Cherry Grove Collections in 2016.

Diane Frank's new book of poems, *Canon for Bears and Ponderosa Pines,* was published in 2018 by Glass Lyre Press. She is editor of the bestselling anthology, *River of Earth and Sky: Poems for the 21st Century,* which is like a box of chocolate for poets. She lives in San Francisco, where she dances, plays cello, and creates her life as an art form. Her Nepal memoir, *Letters from a Sacred Mountain Place: A Journey through the Nepal Himalayas* was published in 2018 by Nirala Publications, with stories, poems and 53 color photographs.

Marc Frazier has widely published poetry in journals including *The Spoon River Poetry Review, ACM, Good Men Project, f(r)iction, Slant, Permafrost, Plainsongs,* and *PoetLore.* He has had memoir published in *Gravel, Autre, The Good Men Project, decomP, Evening Street Review* and forthcoming in *Cobalt Review.* He is the recipient of an Illinois Arts Council Award for poetry and has been featured on *Verse Daily.* His book *The Way Here* and his two chapbooks are available on Amazon as well as his second full-length collection *Each Thing Touches* which has been widely and favorably reviewed. His website is www.marcfrazier.org

Madeline Gardiner is a recent graduate of Northern Michigan University in a place most people think is part of Canada. Her work has been featured or is forthcoming in *Dune's Review* and *Five 2 One Magazine.* She currently works as a tutor and lighthouse tour guide, with plans to attend graduate school within the next few years.

Gail Goepfert an associate editor at *RHINO Poetry*, is a Midwest poet, photographer, and teacher. Her first chapbook, *A Mind on Pain*, was published in 2015. Forthcoming: a chapbook, *Tapping Roots* from Kelsay Books in 2018 and a book, *Get Up Said the World* from Červená Barva, 2019. Recent publications include *Crab Orchard, Jet Fuel, Kudzu House, Rattle, Minerva Rising, Red Paint Hill,* and *Switchgrass Review.*

Grace Marie Grafton is the author of six collections of poetry, most recently *Jester* from Hip Pocket Press. Her themes range from lyrical sonnets to sestinas to experimental prose poems, with a concentration on response to fine art. Her poems have won honors from *The Bellingham Review, Sycamore Review,* Keats Soul Making contest, The National Womens Book Association, and Poetic Matrix Press. Poems recently appear in *Fifth Wednesday, The Cortland Review, Ambush Review, West Trestle Review, Sin Fronteras, Basalt, Mezzo Cammin* and *Poecology,* among others.

Timothy Green has worked as editor of *Rattle* since 2004 and is author of *American Fractal* (Red Hen Press, 2009). He is also co-founder of the Wrightwood Literary Festival and a contributing columnist for the Press-Enterprise (Riverside, CA).

Hedy Habra has authored two poetry collections, *Under Brushstrokes,* finalist for the USA Best Book Award and the International Poetry Book Award, and *Tea in Heliopolis,* winner of the USA Best Book Award and finalist for the International Poetry Book Award. Her story collection, *Flying Carpets,* won the Arab American National Book Award's Honorable Mention and was finalist for the Eric Hoffer Award. A recipient of the Nazim Hikmet Poetry Award, she was a six-time nominee for the Pushcart Prize and Best of the Net. Her work appears in *Cimarron Review, The Bitter Oleander, Blue Fifth Review, Cider Press Review, Drunken Boat, Gargoyle, Nimrod, Poet Lore, World Literature Today* and *Verse Daily.* Her website is <u>hedyhabra.com</u>

Mary Hutchins Harris is a poet and essayist. Her chapbook, *A Tongue Full of Yeses,* was selected by Kwame Dawes for publication in the South Carolina Poetry Initiative/USC Press Chapbook Contest. She has been a featured poet for the Piccolo Spoleto Sundown Series in Charleston, SC. Her work has appeared in *Antietam Review, Kakalak, Main Street Rag, Poemeleon, Pirene's*

Fountain, Spillway, Tar River Poetry, and *Fall Lines/Jaspar Magazine,* as well as in other print and on-line publications. She has taught creative writing and poetry in the Charleston County, SC schools and mentors high school seniors on their Thesis Project for Charleston County School of the Arts. She is an Interdisciplinary Studies Adjunct professor in the Lesley University, Cambridge, MA Low-Residency MFA program.

Melinda B Hipple's poems and short stories have appeared in numerous print and online publications such as *Encore, Watershed, Hillock, Prune Juice, Tinywords* and *Lynx,* and she has been a regular contributor to *Pirene's Fountain.* Three of her poems were anthologized in *First Water: Best of Pirene's Fountain.* She was a past editor and columnist for *Up the Creek News,* and haiga editor for two Japanese short form poetry journals—*Notes from the Gean* and *A Hundred Gourds.* In 2016, she was editor of the annual literary magazine *Watershed.* In addition to poetry, Melinda writes short fiction, creative non-fiction, and mystery and science-fiction novels. Her non-fiction piece "The Cellar" was the first-place winner of the 2014 Moorman Prize for Prose. Her artwork graces the covers of *Floodwater* by Connie Post and *Ribcage* by Joan Colby.

James Croal Jackson is the author of *The Frayed Edge of Memory* (Writing Knights Press, 2017). His poetry has appeared or is forthcoming in *FLAPPERHOUSE, Rust + Moth, The Bitter Oleander,* and elsewhere. He edits *The Mantle.* Find him in Columbus, Ohio or at jimjakk.com.

Trish Lindsey Jaggers, author of *Holonym: a collection of poems* (Finishing Line Press, 2016) and an award-winning Kentucky poet, social activist, feminist, educator, amateur photographer, vintage/antique collector, as well as wife, mother, and grandmother, has published in numerous literary magazines, journals, books, zines, and anthologies. She makes her home on a small farm in Chalybeate, Kentucky and is an assistant professor of English at Western Kentucky University. She want things simple—no impossible-to-connect inferences meant for a limited audience. Her "Crazy-Eights" goal as a poet is to, "Create simply: Write so an eight-year-old can read it, an eighteen-year-old can understand it, and an eighty-year-old will have lived it."

Laurie Kolp's poems have recently appeared in *Stirring, Whale Road Review, concis, Up the Staircase,* and more. Her poetry books include the full-length *Upon the Blue Couch* and chapbook *Hello, It's Your Mother.* An avid runner and lover of nature, Laurie lives in Southeast Texas with her husband, three children, and two dogs. Learn more at http://lauriekolp.com.

Desmond Kon Zhicheng-Mingdé is the author of an epistolary novel, three hybrid works, and nine poetry collections. A former journalist, he has edited more than fifteen books and co-produced three audio books. Among other accolades, Desmond is the recipient of the IBPA Benjamin Franklin Award, Independent Publisher Book Award, National Indie Excellence Book Award, Poetry World Cup, Singapore Literature Prize, two Beverly Hills International Book Awards, and three Living Now Book Awards. Desmond helms Squircle Line Press as its founding editor.

Rustin Larson's fiction has appeared in *Wapsipinicon Almanac, The MacGuffin,* and *The Iowa Source.* His poetry has appeared in *The New Yorker, Iowa Review, North American Review,* and *Poetry East.* He is the author of *Bum Cantos* (Blue Light Press), *The Philosopher Savant* (Glass Lyre Press) and *Pavement,* winner of the Blue Light Poetry Prize for 2016.

Marie C Lecrivain is the editor of *poeticdiversity:* the litzine of Los Angeles, author of several volumes of poetry and fiction, and a writer-in-residence at her apartment. Her work has appeared in *Nonbinary Review, Gargoyle, The Los Angeles Review, Orbis, Spillway,* and various journals. Her new chapbook, *Fourth Planet From the Sun, A 'What If' Tale of an Exiled Ares on Mars,* will be published by Rum Razor Press in Fall 2017.

Peter Ludwin's most recent book is *Gone to Gold Mountain,* a collection based on the Hells Canyon massacre of over thirty Chinese gold miners in 1887 by a gang of horse thieves and school boys. Nominated for a Washington State Book Award, it was subsequently chosen by the Before Columbus Foundation for a 2017 American Book Award. For many years he has participated in the San Miguel Poetry Week in Mexico, where he has studied under such noted poets as Mark Doty, Tony Hoagland, Joseph Stroud and Robert Wrigley. Chosen by Marge Piercy as the 2016 winner of the Muriel Craft Bailey Memorial Award, he works for the Parks Department in Kent, Washington

Dennis Maloney is a poet and translator. A number of volumes of his own poetry have been published including *The Map Is Not the Territory: Poems & Translations* and *Just Enough.* His book *Listening to Tao Yuan Ming* was published by Glass Lyre Press in 2015. A bilingual German/English, *Empty Cup* was recently published in Germany. His works of translation include: *The*

Stones of Chile by Pablo Neruda, *The Landscape of Castile* by Antonio Machado, *Between the Floating Mist: Poems of Ryokan*, and the *The Poet and the Sea* by Juan Ramon Jimenez. He is also the editor and publisher of the widely respected White Pine Press in Buffalo, NY. and divides his time between Buffalo, NY and Big Sur, CA.

Jennifer Martelli's debut poetry collection, *The Uncanny Valley*, was published in 2016 by Big Table Publishing Company. She is also the author of the chapbook, *Apostrophe* and the chapbook, *After Bird*, from Grey Book Press. Her work has appeared in *Thrush, [Pank], Glass Poetry Journal, The Heavy Feather Review*, and *Tinderbox Poetry Journal*. Jennifer Martelli has been nominated for Pushcart and Best of the Net Prizes and is the recipient of the Massachusetts Cultural Council Grant in Poetry. She is a book reviewer for *Up the Staircase Quarterly*, as well as a co-curator for *The Mom Egg VOX Blog Folio*.

Libby Maxey is a senior editor with the online journal *Literary Mama*. She reviews poetry for *The Mom Egg Review* and *Solstice*, and her own poems have appeared in *Mezzo Cammin, Crannóg, Think*, and elsewhere. Her nonliterary activities include singing classical repertoire and mothering two sons.

Ken Meisel is a poet and psychotherapist from the Detroit area. He is a 2012 Kresge Arts Literary Fellow, Pushcart Prize nominee, Swan Duckling chapbook contest winner, winner of the Liakoura Prize and the author of seven poetry collections: *Mortal Lullabies* (FutureCycle Press: 2018), *The Drunken Sweetheart at My Door* (FutureCycle Press: 2015), *Scrap Metal Mantra Poems* (Main Street Rag: 2013), *Beautiful Rust* (Bottom Dog Press: 2009), *Just Listening* (Pure Heart Press: 2007), *Before Exiting* (Pure Heart Press: 2006) and *Sometimes the Wind* (March Street Press: 2002). His work in over 100 national magazines including *Cream City Review, Rattle, Dressing Room Poetry Journal, Midwestern Gothic, Concho River Review, San Pedro River Review, Boxcar Review, Origins Journal, The Bookends Review, Muddy River Poetry Review, Pirene's Fountain, Lake Effect, Soundings East, Gravel Magazine*, and *Lullwater*. He was the featured poet interview in *Rattle* Magazine's September, 2017 Rust Belt Issue.

Cameron Morse lives with his wife Lili and son Theodore in Blue Springs, Missouri. He was diagnosed with a glioblastoma in 2014. With a 14.6 month life expectancy, he entered the Creative Writing program at the University of Missouri—Kansas City and, in 2018, graduated with an M.F.A. His poems have been published in over 100 different magazines, including *New Letters, Bridge Eight*, and *South Dakota Review*. His first collection, *Fall Risk*, won

Glass Lyre Press's 2018 Best Book Award. His second, *Father Me Again*, is forthcoming from Spartan Press.

Robbi Nester is the author of 3 books of poetry, a chapbook, *Balance* (White Violet, 2012) and two collections of poetry: *A Likely Story* (Moon Tide, 2014) and *Other-Wise* (Kelsay Books, 2017). She has also edited two anthologies—*The Liberal Media Made Me Do It!* (Nine Toes, 2014) and an ekphrastic e-anthology, *Over the Moon: Birds, Beasts, and Trees*—celebrating the photography of Beth Moon, which is accessible at http://www.over-the-moon-birds-beasts-and. She has published poems, articles, reviews, and essays in many journals, anthologies, and websites. More information is available at her website, http://www.robbinester-poet-and-writer.com.

Karen Neuberg's latest chapbook is *the elephants are asking* (Glass Lyre Press, 2017). Her poems and collages appear in numerous journals including *Canary, Forage, Poets for Living Waters,* and *S/tick* and anthologies including *First Water: The Best of Pirene's Fountain, A Slant of Light: Contemporary Women Writers of the Hudson Valley,* and *Words Fly Away: Poems for Fukushima.* She's a multiple Pushcart and a Best-of-the-Net nominee, holds an MFA from The New School, and is associate editor of the online poetry journal *First Literary Review East.* She lives in Brooklyn, NY and links to her work can be found at karenneuberg@blogspot.com

Aimee Nezhukumatathil is the author of four books of poetry, most recently, *Oceanic* (Copper Canyon, 2018). With Ross Gay, she co-authored the chapbook, *Lace & Pyrite: Letters from Two Gardens.* Her collection of nature essays is forthcoming from Milkweed. Honors include a Pushcart Prize and a fellowship from the National Endowment for the Arts. She is poetry editor of *Orion* magazine and professor of English in The University of Mississippi's MFA program.

Cristina M. R. Norcross is the founding editor of the online poetry journal, *Blue Heron Review* (www.blueheronreview.com), and the author of 7 poetry collections. Her most recent books include *Amnesia and Awakenings* (Local Gems Press, 2016), and *Still Life Stories* (Aldrich Press, 2016). Her works have been published, or are forthcoming, in: *The Toronto Quarterly, Red Cedar, The Avocet, Your Daily Poem, Lime Hawk, The Poetry Storehouse, Right Hand Pointing,* and *Pirene's Fountain*, among others. Cristina's work also appears in numerous print anthologies. She was a semi-finalist in the 2015 Concrete Wolf Chapbook Competition and a finalist in the 2015 Five Oaks Press Chapbook

Contest. Cristina is currently the co-founder of Random Acts of Poetry and Art Day. Find out more about this poet at: www.cristinanorcross.com

M. Nasorri Pavone's poetry has appeared in *The Cortland Review, River Styx, New Letters, Harpur Palate, The Midwest Quarterly, DMQ Review, La Fovea, Slant, Roanoke Review, Bluestem, Stirring, Chaparral, Green Hills Literary Lantern, Quiddity, Confrontation, Sycamore Review* and elsewhere, with poems upcoming in *Tule Review.* In 2015 Pavone received a Pushcart Prize nomination from *Pirene's Fountain.* The poet's first manuscript made it to semifinals for the Blue Lynx Prize competition and was a finalist for the White Pine Press Poetry Prize. Pavone's work also appears in a recent anthology: *Beyond the Lyric Moment* (Tebot Bach, 2014).

Some of **Jared Pearce**'s poems have recently been or will soon be shared in *Infinity Ink, DIAGRAM, Otoliths, Nixes Mate, Inlandia,* and *MUSE.* He lives in Iowa.

Paul Perreault has traveled through most of the United States, driving stakes and eating fire with two of the three last remaining traditional American carnival sideshows. He has been featured in two Ripley's Believe it or Not's and festivals across the country. When not performing, he leads therapeutic writing workshops within mental health units. He currently lives in Upstate New York and will soon receive a M.A. in Creative Writing from Southern New Hampshire University.

The poet, **Pina Piccolo**, was raised in Italy and Berkeley, presently living in Italy, has a Ph.D. from University of California, Berkeley. A poet, teacher, translator, she edits and publishes *La macchina sognante,* an online journal, http://www.lamacchinasognante.com. That journal's focus, and Piccolo's, is on works in translation, frequently treating issues of immigration, racism, history, and non-European cultural realities, as well as encouraging new literary voices.

Thomas Piekarski is a former editor of the California State Poetry Quarterly and Pushcart Prize nominee. His poetry and interviews have appeared in literary journals internationally, including *Nimrod, Florida English Journal, Cream City Review, Mandala Journal, Poetry Salzburg, Poetry Quarterly, Pennsylvania Literary Journal,* and *Boston Poetry Magazine.*

He has published a travel book, *Best Choices In Northern California* (Gable & Gray), and *Time Lines* (Commentators Press), a book of poems.

Connie Post served as Poet Laureate of Livermore, California (2005 to 2009). Her work has appeared dozens of journals, including *Calyx, Comstock Review, Cold Mountain Review Slipstream, Spillway Spoon River Poetry Review, Valparaiso Poetry Review* and *Verse Daily*. She has written seven books of poetry. Her first full length Book *Floodwater* (Glass Lyre Press 2014) won the Lyrebird Award. Her other awards include the Caesura Award and the 2016 Crab Creek Poetry Award.

Tree Riesener has published widely in print and online. She is the author of *Sleepers Awake*, a collection of fiction, winner of the Eludia Award, Sowilo Press; *The Hubble Cantos,* Aldrich Press; and *EK,* to be published in early 2017 by Cervena Barva Press. She has published three chapbooks: *Liminalog*, a collection of ghazals and sijo, *Inscapes,* from Finishing Line Press, and *Angel Poison,* from Pudding House Publications. She is former Managing Editor of the *Schuylkill Valley Journal* and former Contributing Editor to *The Ghazal Page*. Her website is http://www.treeriesener.com. She is on Facebook and Twitter, and she loves to hear from readers.

Claire Donohue Roof is an assistant professor of English at Ivy Tech Community College. She has been published in *Common Ground Review, TheDeepLiterary Journal,* and *CaKe* literary journal. She edited the college's creative writing and arts magazine, *The Ivy Quill,* for the first six editions. She has placed first place in the Advocate Magazine's poetry contest in Hartford, Connecticut for her poem, Homesick.

Beate Sigriddaughter, www.sigriddaughter.com, is poet laureate of Silver City, New Mexico (Land of Enchantment). Her work has received several Pushcart Prize nominations and poetry awards. In 2018 FutureCycle Press will publish her poetry collection *Xanthippe and Her Friends* and Červená Barva Press will publish her chapbook *Dancing in Santa Fe and Other Poems* in 2019.

Joannie Stangeland is the author of *In Both Hands* and *Into the Rumored Spring* from Ravenna Press, and three chapbooks. Her poems have also appeared in *Prairie Schooner, The Southern Review, Mid-American Review,* and other journals. Joannie has been a Jack Straw writer, and she is currently enrolled in the MFA program at Rainier Writing Workshop.

Tim Suermondt is the author of three full-length collections of poems: *Trying To Help The Elephant Man Dance* (The Backwaters Press, 2007), *Just Beautiful* (New York Quarterly Books, 2010) and *Election Night And The Five Satins* (Glass Lyre Press, 2016.)—Pinyon Publishing will publish his fourth full-length collection *The World Doesn't Know You* later in 2017 and MadHat Press will publish his fifth full-length collection, *Josephine Baker Swimming Pool*. He has poems published in *Poetry, The Georgia Review, Ploughshares, Prairie Schooner, Blackbird, Bellevue Literary Review, North Dakota Quarterly, december magazine, Plume Poetry Journal, Poetry East* and *Stand Magazine* (England), among others. He is a book reviewer for Cervena Barva Press and a poetry reviewer for *Bellevue Literary Review*. He lives in Cambridge (MA) with his wife, the poet Pui Ying Wong.

Susan Tepper is the author of seven published books of fiction and poetry. Her most recent title *Monte Carlo Days & Nights* is a Novella set in the South of France. Tepper has received many awards and honors including a Pultizer Prize Nomination for her novel *What May Have Been*. For more please visit www.susantepper.com

Jon Tribble is author of three collections of poems: *Natural State* (Glass Lyre Press, 2016), *And There Is Many a Good Thing* (Salmon Poetry, 2017), and *God of the Kitchen* (Glass Lyre Press, 2018). He is the recipient of a 2003 Artist Fellowship Award in Poetry from the Illinois Arts Council and his poems have appeared in journals and anthologies, including *Ploughshares, Poetry, Crazyhorse, Quarterly West,* and *The Jazz Poetry Anthology*. His work was selected as the 2001 winner of the Campbell Corner Poetry Prize from Sarah Lawrence College. He is managing editor of *Crab Orchard Review* and series editor of the Crab Orchard Series in Poetry published by SIU Press.

Editor-In-Chief of *Cutthroat, A Journal Of The Arts*, **Pam Uschuk** lives in Tucson, Arizona. Political activist and wilderness advocate, Uschuk has howled out six books of award-winning poems, including *Crazy Love,*

Finding Peaches In The Desert, and *Blood Flower*. Translations of her work appear in over three hundred journals and anthologies worldwide. She edited the anthology, *Truth To Power: Writers Respond To The Rhetoric Of Hate And Fear*, 2017. Among her awards are the New Millenium Poetry Prize, Best of the Web, the King's English Poetry Prize and prizes from Ascent, Iris, and Amnesty International. Uschuk is often a featured writer at the Prague Summer Programs and at Ghost Ranch. She was the 2011 John C. Hodges Visiting Writer at University of Tennessee, Knoxville. She is finishing work on a multi-genre book called *Of Thunderlight and Moon: An Odyssey Through Ovarian Cancer*. In June 2018, Uschuk was named a Black Earth Institute Fellow for 2018-2021.

Helen Wickes worked for many years as a psychotherapist and received an MFA from the Bennington Writing Seminars in 2002. Glass Lyre Press published her second and third books—*The Moon Over Zabriskie* and *Dowser's Apprentice*—in 2014. Sixteen Rivers Press published *The World As You Left It* in 2015.

Martin Willitts Jr. won the 2014 Dylan Thomas International Poetry Award; and, *Rattle* Ekphrastic Challenge, June 2015, Editor's Choice. He has over 20 chapbooks including the winner of the Turtle Island Quarterly Editor's Choice Award, *The Wire Fence Holding Back the World* (Flowstone Press), plus 11 full-length collections including *Dylan Thomas and the Writing Shed* (FutureCycle Press, 2017).

Kath Abela Wilson lived and wrote mainly in Santa Barbara, Califilornia for 30 years, and still maintains a residence there, where the Ocean infuses her poetry with salty enigmatic inspiration. She lived for years on a street that led to stairs to the sea and walked there every day. Her poems and art are intimately linked with the tides, waves, stones and driftwood. Her free verse, and Asian short form poetry is published in hundreds of journals worldwide. She travels the world with her husband Rick, a math professor and historical and world flute collector and player, performing together. She hosts poetry meetings and salons at her home, and local gardens and museums.

Recently her haiku was honored with third place in The Santoka International Haiku Contest, 2017 "Peace", and honorable mention in the Yuki Teikei Haiku Society Haiku Contest, 2017, and British Haiku Society Contest, 2017. Her tanka won first place in English language Tanka in the Fujisan Contest, 2017. She is secretary of the Tanka Society of America.

Bill Yarrow, Professor of English at Joliet Junior College and an editor at *Blue Fifth Review,* is the author of *The Vig of Love, Blasphemer, Pointed Sentences,* and five chapbooks, most recently *We All Saw It Coming.* He has been nominated eight times for a Pushcart Prize. Two new full-length collections, *Accelerant* (Nixes Mate Books) and *Against Prompts* (Lit Fest Press) are forthcoming in fall 2018.

The Aeolian Harp Series, Volume 4

GUEST EDITOR
MELISSA STUDDARD OF *VIDA VOICES & VIEWS*

Featuring
Cynthia Atkins
Susan Berlin
Raymond Gibson
Shadab Zeest Hashmi
Jocelyn Heath
Tanya Ko Hong
John James
Jennifer Martelli
Pamela Uschuk
Mark Lee Webb

Available Now!

"Steffen Horstmann's ghazals illuminate the form's potential in English."

–Gene Doty, Editor, *The Ghazal Page*

Jalsaghar

STEFFEN HORSTMANN

Available now on Amazon!

"*My hands memorize your hourglass waist. / Slow winds pass through distant sands, sifting grains.* Imagine that beauty rethought in stanza after stanza. The ghazal is the Satie of poetry, sustained by the whirling dervish, its couplets braiding into the brain. Steffen Horstmann's Jalsaghar is a stunning homage to the late Agha Shahid Ali."

—**Terese Svoboda,** author of *Professor Harriman's Steam Air-Ship*

"A rapprochement with a formal tradition demands incisive cultural evaluation; an assay of a formal tradition "no one's own" demands that one become a naturalized citizen of a nation of poetry. The sure-footedness with which Steffen Horstmann navigates the ghazal form — a kind of poem often misunderstood in Anglophone practice — is a testimony to long and devoted study as well as to Horstmann's skill as a practitioner, his keen ear, and his passion for the possibilities of the kind of détente poetry offers: a genuine cross-pollination of the music, the landscapes, the souls of distant and yet always kindred lives."

—**T.R. Hummer,** author of *Skandalon*

"Steffen Horstmann's book of contemporary ghazals shows us the ways in which form — in this case precise, musical, devotional in its origins— can act as a vehicle for meditation. The rhymes and repetitions of the ghazal are part prayer, part spell, and as such they bind together in language the world of material things and the world of spirit, which is also a world of lonnging. Agha Shahid Ali brought the tradition of the ghazal into the center of our contemporary and American poetic repertoire; Steffen Horstmann has carried it into our young century, made it new."

—**Mark Wunderlich,** author of *The Earth Avails*

Available now on Amazon!

"Steffen Horstmann's book *Ujjain* is a remarkable collection of ghazals in English. Steffen uses an ancient form of poetry to express the sensibility of a modern day poet, and by doing so he crosses the boundaries of languages, cultures, and traditions. Agha Shahid Ali couldn't have been more proud of his *Shagird* Steffen Horstmann, who has kept the torch burning, that he passed to him after writing *Call Me Ishmael Tonight*."

—**Kalpna Singh-Chitnis**, author of *Bare Soul*

"The meditative and sublime states in Steffen Horstmann's radiant collection *Ujjain* render sonorous arias of cautionary tales for our time—those places of beauty, loss, and pain collide into longing for a vanished world. In these astute ghazals, myth and life and after-life send this poet on a path to claim where 'the self' fits in: "Of a world that vanished before I existed." Horstmann's luminous voice guides us to where beauty resides, "through the dark like a train there," — these evocations torque into epiphanies rich with awe to light our way — and we are so much richer for this journey.

—**Cynthia Atkins**, author of *In the Event of Full Disclosure*

"Steffen Horstmann is a worthy student of Agha Shahid Ali in this collection of ghazals which embraces the East and West, as much at ease on Arjuna's chariot as among the sacred tombs of Ithaka, or the very real foothils of Qhar. The natural world is incandescent: "Bass glisten in rock pools like slick knives / With silver light glinting in their fast shadows," but it is *The Diva Jalsaghar* that elegantly soars on melody as "Air is scriptured by the syllabic flight / Of the voice of Begum Akhtar." A thoughtful and lyrical collection of ghazals written in English."

—**Dipika Mukherjee,** author of *Shambala Junction*

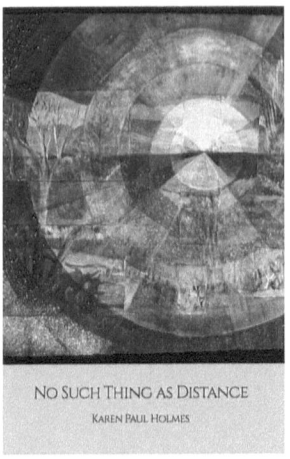

No Such Thing as Distance
by Karen Paul Holmes / $16

Aileron
by Geraldine Connolly / $16

How to Wear This Body
by Hayden Saunier / $16

The Infinite Doctrine of Water
by Michael T. Young / $16

Terrapin Books

Titles available from Amazon, B&N, and wherever books are sold.

**Open for submissions of full-length poetry manuscripts August 1 - 31.
See our website for Guidelines
www.terrapinbooks.com**

NEW! Available September 2018

Includes craft lessons by 30 poets such as Barbara Hamby, Campbell McGrath, & Pattiann Rogers; 30 model poems by such poets as Thomas Lux, Ada Limon, & Peter Everwine. Plus 40 prompts. Plus Top Tips Lists from such poets as Patricia Smith, Jan Beatty, & David Kirby.

Terrapin Books
www.terrapinbooks.com
ISBN:
$21.00 / 300 pages
Available from Amazon, B&N, and wherever books are sold

The Girl & The Fox Pirate

Stories by
Kate Gehan

Kate Gehan's stunning debut collection of short fiction, available in print and as an ebook from major online retailers September 2018

"These stories are by turns searing, delightful, and heartbreaking. *The Girl and the Fox Pirate* is a collection by a writer in full command of her craft. Highly recommended."

—**Kathy Fish,** author of *Together We Can Bury It*

"Reminiscent of Jayne Anne Phillips' Black Tickets, these are stories and poems at the same time – brief, lyrical glimpses into the richest interior worlds. Gehan's sentences are crystals, beautiful and sharp, revealing hidden facets of ordinary people in a uniquely brilliant light. A sparkling debut."

—**Jessica Treadway,** author of *Lacy Eye* and *How Will I Know You?*

MOJAVE RIVER PRESS

Glass Lyre Press

exceptional works to replenish the spirit

Glass Lyre Press is an independent literary publisher interested in technically accomplished, stylistically distinct, and original work. Glass Lyre seeks diverse writers that possess a dynamic aesthetic and an ability to emotionally and intellectually engage a wide audience of readers.

Glass Lyre's vision is to connect the world through language and art. We hope to expand the scope of poetry and short fiction for the general reader through exceptionally well-written books, which evoke emotion, provide insight, and resonate with the human spirit.

Poetry Collections
Poetry Chapbooks
Select Short & Flash Fiction
Anthologies

www.GlassLyrePress.com

www.ingramcontent.com/pod-product-compliance
Lightning Source LLC
Chambersburg PA
CBHW030117100526
44591CB00009B/434